MARCO  POLO

Travel with
**Insider
Tips**

SARDINIA

GERMANY

SWITZERLAND   AUSTRIA

FRANCE   ○ Milan
                        SLO.
AND.   **ITALY**   CROATIA
                        BOSNIA-
SPAIN   RSM   HERZEG.
        Corsica   ○ Rome
        (F)

        Sardinia (I)
        Mediterranean Sea   Sicily

ALGERIA

        TUNISIA

D1448606

www.marco-polo.com

The best Insider Tips → p. 4

INSIDER TIP

Best of ... → p. 6

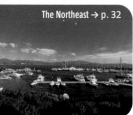

The Northeast → p. 32

The Northwest → p. 44

SYMBOLS

INSIDER TIP	Insider Tip
★	Highlight
●●●●	Best of ...
☆	Scenic view
☺	Responsible travel: fair trade principles and the environment respected
(*)	Telephone numbers that are not toll-free

PRICE CATEGORIES HOTELS

Expensive	over 100 euros
Moderate	80–100 euros
Budget	under 80 euros

Prices are valid for two people in a double room per night without breakfast

PRICE CATEGORIES RESTAURANTS

Expensive	over 50 euros
Moderate	30–50 euros
Budget	under 30 euros

Prices are valid for a meal with starter or pasta dish, main dish, side dishes, dessert and house wine

On the cover: Europe's highest dunes p. 68 | Murals in the shepherd's village of Orgosolo p. 93

CONTENTS

The South → p. 58

DID YOU KNOW?
Timeline → p. 12
Quattro Mori → p. 20
Local specialities → p. 26
Books & Films → p. 57
Family feuds → p. 92
Budgeting → p. 113
Weather in Cagliari → p. 114
Currency converter → p. 115
Pronunciation → p. 116

MAPS IN THE GUIDEBOOK
(124 A1) Page numbers and
coordinates refer to the road
atlas
(0) Site/address located off
the map
Coordinates are also given for
places that are not marked
on the road atlas
Maps of Cagliari, Nuoro,
Olbia and Sassari can be
found in the back cover

INSIDE BACK COVER:
PULL-OUT MAP →

PULL-OUT MAP 🗺
(🗺 A–B 2–3) Refers to the
removable pull-out map

The best MARCO POLO Insider Tips

Our top 15 Insider Tips

INSIDERTIP Double pleasure: eating and cycling

Sole e Terra – sun and earth – is an organic agriturismo in the quiet countryside near Santa Teresa, offering fine cuisine with many vegetarian dishes as well as exclusive mountain biking and road cycling tours through the Gallura → p. 43

INSIDERTIP Europe's oldest tree

Incredible: the wild olive tree on Lago di Liscia has been around for 4000–4500 years. Compared to this ancient giant, the two other olive trees are mere upstarts, at only 1000 and 2500 years of age → p. 38

INSIDERTIP Phew!

In the Sant'Antine church near Sedilo the faithful have hung up countless naïve votive images, in gratitude for their salvation, making up an eccentric and tragicomic gallery → p. 73

INSIDERTIP At grandmother's table

You'll find a welcoming ambience and traditional Sardinian cuisine at the Trattoria Zia Giovanna in Padria → p. 51

INSIDERTIP Horse parade in colourful costumes

The cavalcata sarda in Sassari is a large colourful procession with Sardinian costumes and traditions (photo right) → p. 108

INSIDERTIP At home with the dolphins

A boat excursion to the playful dolphins in La Maddalena National Park is a unique experience → p. 35

INSIDERTIP Eye to eye with griffon vultures

A guided trip to the cliffs of Capo Marargiu, one of the last remaining vulture colonies in Europe, is the closest you'll ever get to these giants of the air → p. 51

BEST OF ...

FOR FREE

● *Natural cave*
The *Grotta di San Giovanni,* at Domusnovas, is a unique natural tunnel dug into the mountain by a brook. The tunnel was used as a road (now closed to traffic) and you may walk through it for free → p. 68

● *Capo Testa*
Completely free of charge and freely accessible, this cape at Santa Teresa di Gallura is a fairy-tale world of whimsical rock formations that would take days to explore. Don't forget your towel so you can make use of the idyllic beach coves → p. 43

● *Free history: Museo Francesco Bande in Sassari*
This free museum will teach you about a subject close to the heart of Sardinians: it commemorates a great Sardinian singer and accordion player whose songs made him an immortal presence in Sardinian musical history → p. 54

● *Cork Museum*
Wine bottles sealed with natural cork are on the wane. Those wanting to find out more about this versatile and ancient natural product, should visit the *Museo delle Macchine del Sughero* in Tempio Pausania – admission is free → p. 39

● *Mountains in the nature reserve*
Marked trails, with picnic spots, lead through the wild, romantic mountainous *Parco Sette Fratelli*. An information centre at the entrance has route maps, and the free Museo Cervo Sardo provides information about the rare endemic Sardinian deer → p. 75

● *A village as an open air gallery*
The most famous village of murals is the shepherd's village of *Orgosolo*. Walking around Orgosolo is like visiting a large open air gallery (photo) → p. 93

ONLY IN SARDINIA
Unique experiences

● *Pecorino and pane Carasau*
The paper-thin flatbread and aromatic sheep's cheese are the staple fare of local shepherds and in the mountains and the island's interior, both are often still made by hand following time-honoured traditions, e.g. on the *agriturismo* farm of *Costiolu* near Nuoro → p. 89

● *Vermentino and Cannonau*
Over the past decade, Sardinian winemakers have taken an enormous leap forward in terms of quality, producing some excellent red and white wines which have achieved international cult status. The most exclusive Vermentino is the *Capichera* produced by the eponymous estate near Arzachena → p. 27

● *Fairy houses*
Everywhere on Sardinia you'll spot large and small cave openings – so-called *domus de janas,* or 'fairy houses' – these are prehistoric burial tombs hewn into the rock. One of the most impressive is the extensive *Montessu necropolis,* stretching across two hills. You can walk for hours on the trails that run through the peaceful countryside: or even crawl into the numerous grottoes and burial vaults → p. 67

● *Shepherd's knife*
Every boy longs to have one and every Sardinian proudly carries it with him – the pocketknife used by the Sardinian shepherds. In the past, nearly every village had its own cutler, today there are only few villages left that continue this art; such as *Arbus* and *Pattada* → p. 29

● *Boat trip in the La Maddalena national park*
What better activity to do on an island than a boat trip? The most beautiful destinations are the numerous islets and beaches in the national park between Sardinia and Corsica (photo) → p. 41

● *Dine alfresco*
A shepherd's dinner in the open air is always a special experience. Do as the Sardinians do and take your own picnic – *Monte Ortobene* above Nuoro is a popular spot → p. 91

ONLY IN

BEST OF ...

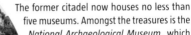

● *Cagliari's citadel museums*
The former citadel now houses no less than five museums. Amongst the treasures is the *National Archaeological Museum*, which promises an exciting trip through the prehistory and early history of the island → p. 60

● *Museo Etnografico Nuoro*
Immerse yourself in the rich traditions and folk art of the Sardinians. In addition to the fabulous collection of costumes – every village has its very own – there is an exhibition about Sardinian bread that illustrates the particular significance of bread with more than 600 exhibits → p. 89

● *Trenino Verde*
The island was once criss-crossed by a network of narrow gauge railway tracks. Today some of the most beautiful sections are run (in season) for tourists – an unforgettable day trip is the journey from Sassari to Tempio Pausania (photo) → p. 55

● *Fordongianus thermal baths*
Even the ancient Romans knew to appreciate the relaxing thermal springs. Pay a small fee and luxuriate in the hot water – 43 °C / 109 °F – of the *Bagni Termali Comunali*, built around 1800 → p. 74

● *Museum of Sardinian Knives*
A visit to the *Museo del Coltello Sardo,* in a historic forge in Arbus, offers a good opportunity to watch how a knife is actually made → p. 106

● *In the belly of the mountain*
Sardinia is an island of caves. Escape the rain and go diving down – there are dive sites all over the island, such as the *Grotta di Ispingoli* at Dorgali on the east coast → p. 82

RAIN

RELAX AND CHILL OUT
Take it easy and spoil yourself

● *Beach village Santa Maria Navarrese*
This flower-bedecked seaside resort on the Gulf of Orosei has miles of sandy beaches. Sit under an ancient olive tree right on the beach – if you can't relax here, you won't relax anywhere → p. 78

● *Natural pool with goldfish*
Leave the coast behind for a picnic and freshwater swim in the country-side, with birdsong and gently whispering leaves. A highlight is the *piscina naturale* – formed by the Riu Flumendosa at Ballao – swimming with goldfish that were released into the wild → p. 98

● *Sunset in the Al 906 Operaio rock bar*
This bar is in a cavern in Nebida that was once used as a storeroom for mine dynamite. Enjoy the sunset view of the sublimely dramatic coast from the terrace → p. 68

● *Moonlight concert*
To experience the *Notte dei Poeti* – at the ancient theatre in the old Roman city of Nora – on a mild summer's night under the broad canopy of stars, overlooking the glittering sea, is unforgettable → p. 64

● *Trip on the paddle steamer*
In season, this Mississippi paddle steamer offers the opportunity for a romantic journey across the large Lago di Flumendosa reservoir lake → p. 99

● *Secluded beaches*
The miles of sandy beaches on the *Costa Rei* are not yet overwhelmed by tourists and there are still some that you will have entirely to yourself (photo) → p. 74

● *Siesta at the cool spring*
Oliena's *Su Gologone* spring is a lush, green, shady oasis that feeds into the clear waters of the Cedrino brook that runs through it. Particularly beautiful: as dusk falls, the nightingales start to sing! → p. 92

INTRODUCTION

DISCOVER SARDINIA!

An island with many mountains, surrounded by the deep blue sea – Sardinia, let's not forget, is the second-largest island in the Mediterranean and one of the world's tourist hotspots. And yet, somehow this spot on the planet is still often overlooked, unknown to many, foreign even, and a little mysterious – which makes the place all the more intriguing.

Naturally, Sardinia, with its Mediterranean climate and nearly 2000km/1242mi of coast – blessed with countless picture-perfect beaches and coves – is most of all a beautiful island for a beach holiday. It can easily be compared to the Caribbean or the South Sea Islands and has everything that's required for a perfect beach holiday. But Sardinia is about a lot more than just beaches: the wild world of Sardinia's mountains and unspoilt nature is a paradise for hikers and mountain bikers, for mountaineers and climbers, but also for amateur botanists and herbalists, as many of the plants on the island are endemic, i.e. only occur here in Sardinia. Visitors soon find out that this 'small continent in the Mediterranean' is far too varied to be captured

Photo: Beach on the Costa del Sud

in a single stay: stroll through the jagged granite landscape of the Gallura or the limestone rocks of the Supramonte; hike across the wild and wind-swept Marmilla plateau or through the densely forested mountains of the Gennargentu, which often appear more like the Scottish Highlands than a Mediterranean mountain range. Stroll along the volcanic coastal cliffs of Costa Paradiso, whose bizarre shapes and colours are like the backdrop from a science fiction film, or trundle through the expanse of the Sarcidano, reminiscent of the steppes of Africa ...

> **Each village has its own costume, cuisine and festivals**

The further you move away from the coast, the more the 'real' Sardinia emerges: quiet isolated ancient pilgrimage churches, unkempt mountain villages with steep and narrow lanes, huddled on the slopes, subterranean well sanctuaries or overgrown nuraghi – mystic relics of the Stone Age Nuragic civilization. And your constant companion heard from near or far, is the 'sound of Sardinia': the high-pitched jingling from the bells of the herds of sheep and goats, which roam the deserted landscape only accompanied by their sheepdog.

The best time to experience Sardinia is in May and June, when temperatures are already summery, yet the countryside is still a lush green with plenty of blossoms, and the air is still fresh and clear. From mid June, temperatures rise dramatically, and the dry heat withers the vegetation. But autumn is also beautiful: while September is still dry and summery, from about mid October the first rains arrive, lending the island a second spring coat of greenery and flowers. The sea is still warm, and you can swim up to late October.

Yet all this would not be complete without the people who inhabit this fascinating natural world. An encounter with a shepherd or a winemaker, a chef or a bar owner is at least as much a part of the experience that is Sardinia. Their restrained pride and unrivalled hospitality reflect Sardinia's character as much as their archaic songs, the exotic melodies of the *launedda* (shepherd's flute) or the melancholic yet fiery *ballu tundu,* the circle folk dance.

Around 6000 BC
The first settlers of northern Sardinia arrive from Corsica

From 1800 BC
The Nuragic people reach the island

From 700 BC
Phoenicians from North Africa begin building cities, displacing the Nuragic

238 BC
Sardinia becomes a Roman province and remains part of the Roman Empire until its collapse

Around 900 AD
Four autonomous regions, or giudicati are formed, with a judge each at the helm: Arborea, Cagliari, Gallura and Torres

Sanctuary of the Roman-Punic blend of cultures: Temple of Antas in Iglesias

Chi venit de è su mare furat – 'Those who come across the sea come to steal': this ancient Sardinian saying characterises the island. Since the landing of the Phoenicians, the first conquerors from the 8th century onwards, who arrived to exploit the valuable ore mines in the south-west of Sardinia, the small island has been prey to foreign rulers, who wanted nothing more but to enslave the local population and the exploit the riches of the island. The Sardinians retreated from the coasts into the wild and inaccessible mountains, turning their back on the sea and the world. This explains why the Sardinians even today have a reputation with their fellow Italians of being backward, reticent and withdrawn – they were even called robbers and bandits until well into the 20th century.

> **A 'small continent in the Mediterranean'**

1297
The Pope gives Sardinia to the Spanish royal dynasty of Aragón

1478–1708
Sardinia is part of the Spanish global empire. The rural population sinks into serfdom

1820
Passing of the fateful edict ordering land enclosures (one that still impacts on agriculture to this day): the large common pastures are taken over by the wealthy and enclosed with walls

1926
Nuoro-born writer Grazia Deledda (1871–1936) is awarded the Nobel Prize for Literature

The upside of this is that it inspired Sardinians to cherish their ancient traditions even more; as with other threatened groups, this is ensured the safeguarding of their own identity. For centuries, they resisted all conquerors from their inaccessible mountain lairs. Poor but proud, unyielding and free – those were their attributes then and so they have remained today. The Romans called them 'barbarians', and to this day the interior around Nuoro bears the name 'Nuoro Barbagia'. The island with its malaria-infested coasts became a dreaded place of exile. From the ancient Romans up until the end of the Mussolini era in the 1940s, undesirables were deported to Sardinia.

A population that holds hospitality sacred

Over time, the Sardinians became a people of farmers and shepherds, whose villages remained so lonely and isolated until far into the 20th century that countless local dialects emerged, making it impossible even for locals to mutually understand themselves. This is also the root of Sardinia's immense wealth of customs and traditions: every village has its own distinctive costume, music, cuisine, festivals and rituals.

Today, this millennia-long seclusion is the island's greatest asset, while all around the Mediterranean booming mass tourism covered the coasts in concrete, turned fishermen into snack bar owners and degraded tradition and culture to a cheap spectacle for tourists, Sardinia remained on the sidelines in splendid isolation. When the Aga Khan, one of the world's richest people, brought tourism to the island, in the early 1960s with his legendary Costa Smeralda, he broke into an archaic world which was still governed by the traditional principles of honour, family and community rather than by laws made in distant Rome.

The Costa Smeralda and the few other tourist centres that slowly developed along the Gallura coast in the north and the southern Costa Rei remained for a long time isolated worlds that had little to do with Sardinia or the Sardinians – and the season was short, only six weeks. Those few visitors that succumbed to the charm and magic of this forgotten island in those early days faced a long, expensive and complicated journey – as recently as the 1970s cars were loaded into the belly of ferries by crane, and direct flights from abroad are also relatively new.

1948 Sardinia becomes an autonomous region within the Republic of Italy

1998 The La Maddalena archipelago off the northern coast becomes Sardinia's first national park

2005 The island has a new administrative structure, dividing it into eight rather than four provinces

2006 Sardinian becomes the island's second official language

2009 In the regional elections, the centre-right coalition Ugo Cappellacci, takes office as President of the island, replacing the left-leaning Renato Soru

It was only with the advent of the low-cost airlines that Sardinia was gradually discovered as a holiday destination. And what a destination it is! Largely untouched by the excesses of mass tourism (no overdeveloped coasts and urban sprawl) Sardinia offers one pristine beach after another and a wonderful, enormously varied nature, which immediately showcases the epithet of 'a small continent in the Mediterranean'. Add to this a popula-

> **Beaches that compare well to those in the Caribbean**

tion deeply rooted in their traditions, and rather restrained too – in this respect Sardinians have little in common with the extrovert Italian hotheads from the mainland – but one that holds hospitality dear and makes it a point of honour to treat guests with integrity and respect.

And last but not least, there is the Sardinian cuisine and art of cooking! As much pride and dedication as the Sardinians put into looking after their traditions, is matched by the attention and love they give to their cuisine, which, by the way, you'll get to know better in the interior than on the coast. It is not uncommon for visitors there to be spontaneously invited to a family feast or a village festival, and to be given a warm welcome into the community. And there is no lack of opportunities really, as every day an average of 2.7 festivals regularly takes place on the island, resulting in the substantial figure of over 1000 each year. You need only experience one such village festival – in celebration of the harvest, sheep-shearing, saints or tournaments – to really touch the heart of Sardinia. When the stubble bearded shepherds start singing their old songs, accompanied by the heavy red Cannonau, when the accordion player gets going and everyone starts dancing in a *ballu tundu* circle, folding in strangers with natural ease – that is when you too will fall for this island, an island that is as singular as it is wonderful – and you will be sure to come back soon.

Sweet inside, prickly outside: the fruit of the cactus fig

WHAT'S HOT

1 Porto Cervo Harbour

Cultural village Pop-up shops, cosy cafés, galleries and trendy bars. The *Promenade du Port (www.promenadeduport.com)* is Porto Cervo's hippest boulevard to see and be seen. Every summer you'll encounter cool furniture designs by *Rossana Orlandi (www.rossanaorlandi.com)* or contemporary art in galleries such as *Fumi (www.galleryfumi.com)* and *Louise Alexander (www.louise-alexander.com)*. A classy refreshment option is the *Ruinart Champagneria* on the third floor above the MdM Museum. Sea views are included!

Creative island 2

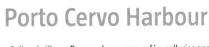

Variety Off the mainland, Sardinia's artists are developing their very own style. One of them is *Gavino Ganau (www.gavinoganau.com, photo)*, who blends black and white photography and painting. For those who enjoy experimental art, there is 'Project Space' *Askos Arte (Via Trento 16, www.askosarte. it)* in Solarussa near Oristano. Here, the island's artists explore their creative instincts and showcase their work. More examples of the scene at the *La Bacheca gallery (Via dei Pisani 1)* in Cagliari.

3 Good vibes

Dub Sardinia's DJs are taking reggae back on to the dance floor – as a danceable dub version. Remixes by *Arrogalla (www.myspace. com/arrogalla, photo)* use not only Jamaican rhythms, but also Sardinian beats, making him the darling of the locals. One of the venues where the DJ is on the turntables is *Club Caracol (Via San Giovanni 251, www.myspace.com/caracolclubcagli ari)* in Cagliari. Another excellent place to listen to dub is the *Z-One Fashion Club (Via Ghilarza, www.zone-fashionclub.it)* in Oristano.

Dual sports

2 in 1 When it comes to sports, the region has a lot to offer. So why not combine two favourite sports and keep the whole body fit with a variety of exercise? That is the concept behind *Yoga on the Rock (photo)* and their courses around Cala Gonone. First step into the warrior position and then scramble up the cliff. If you'd rather learn to kayak and then do a hike, try a nature hike and kayaking session with *Sea Kayak Sardinia (www.seakayaksardinia.com)*. Or would you rather take a flexible approach to the sporty dimension of your stay? The *Nyce Club Sport Village (in Baia delle Mimose, www.nyceclub.it)* in Badesi on the northern coast offers a huge range of sports to choose from.

4

Organic Sardegna

5

Back to the roots Had enough of Sardinia's glamorous side? Then tuck in at one of the many *agriturismi*. The 🕙 *Cucchè* organic farm *(www.bio-farmcucche.it, photo)* in Dorgali serves a new, typically Sardinian menu every evening, using the produce from the farm. Particularly tasty: the braised meats. The 🕙 *Agriturismo Biologico Santa Lucia (www.agrislucia.it)* in Tratalias near Carbonia also serves authentic Sardinian cuisine using seasonal produce. Suckling pig roasted over hot coals, sweet ravioli with raisins, a salad with chestnuts: at *Sa Corte (Via Nuoro, www.sacorte.it)* in Oliena, lovers of the island's cuisine will be in heaven.

IN A NUTSHELL

A UTONOMY

Graffiti alongside the roadside proclaims: *A foras sos Italianos* – Italians out. Luckily, things aren't as hot as on the neighbouring island of Corsica, and the frustration about being patronised by Rome has not erupted into violence. Here, it's still *murales* talking instead of bombs. They are demanding what the South Tyroleans already enjoy, autonomy in matters of education, culture and finance and the right to their own language. The regional government in Cagliari had no say in the arrival of large (and not exactly green) industries, nor in the creation of the huge military exclusion areas which have turned Sardinia into an 'unsinkable aircraft carrier' brimming with electronics and weapons.

Hardly anybody is seriously considering the creation of a small (and certainly not viable) State of Sardinia.

B EACHES

Every single holidaymaker probably heads first to Sardinia's beaches. There are in fact so many of them – and they are so beautiful – that the comparison with the Caribbean islands is by no mean an exaggeration. Sardinia boasts 1870km/1660mi of coastline. A good few miles of those are inaccessible cliffs, while most consists of beaches, many of them still completely undiscovered. Apart from a few scrappy areas around the large ports and industrial zones (Cagliari to Sarroch, Portovesme and Porto Torres), the sea is very clean

Why the Sardinians are no Italians: notes on autonomy, nuraghi, sheep and the Sardinian language

and many beaches are pristine. The northern and western coasts are exposed to wind, the eastern and southern coastlines are much calmer, yet even here you can expect the occasional stiff breeze. The swimming season starts in May, with hardy souls wading in earlier. The pleasant water temperatures continue into October, reaching, in warm years, 18 °C /64 °F far into November.

Many beaches are not signposted and are difficult to find. One way of identifying your personal favourite amongst this wealth of options, ranging from secluded Robinson Crusoe bays to the endless wide sandy beaches, is to consult the *www.sardinianplaces.co.uk* webpage with its extensive information on the beaches of Sardinia. Published by the Legambiente environmental organisation and updated every year, the Guida Blu *(www.legambiente.it/guidablu-2012)* awards its seal of quality to dozens of beaches. The beaches of Domus de Maria on the Costa del Sud, Baunei on the central eastern coast, and Posada, also on the east coast, at Siniscola south of San Teodoro, as well as Budoni hold top positions.

CATHEDRALS IN THE DESERT

This phrase hits the nail on the head, describing all those big industrialisation projects which were used by politicians and state institutions to promise a fast turnaround of problematic areas, and nearly always only served to fill the pockets and promote the careers of friends of friends. The planners in Rome don't really have much time for small co-ops and family-run businesses. The more propitious choice for electioneering are huge facilities such as the large petroleum refineries in Porto Torres and the Gulf of Cagliari, the chemical fibre plant at Ottana or the paper factory at Arbatax. All those have created few jobs, import their raw materials from outside and produce little for the Sardinian market, pollute the environment and are more or less being threatened by closure.

CONSERVATION

A double-edged sword in Sardinia. While enormous progress has been made on the part of the state, most Sardinians' ecological awareness leaves a lot to be desired: disregard for the maquis, lots of scrapped cars, fridges and TV sets. An inordinate number of families eat using only disposable plates and cutlery, which are then simply burnt in the kitchen stove, together with a lot of other things. The annual forest fires that destroy precious greenery often occur because of careless handling of fire, with some even being set deliberately. Many cooperatives founded by young Sardinians attempt to actively foment the development of an ecological awarenss through educational and training campaigns.

The state is doing its part by taking requisite measures. Separating the rubbish for recycling is now obligatory across the island (including holidaymakers!), and even the most remote beach car park now has refuse bins. Violations of conservation orders, open fires and illegal rubbish dumping all attract heavy fines. Another positive initiative taken by the region is the establishment of numerous large protected areas on water and on land, which are now supervised as well, after going unchecked for years.

QUATTRO MORI

The official coat of arms for Sardinia, the Four Moors, is a red cross on a white background with a moor's head in each corner. It is a mystery as to why they ended up on the coat of arms and why it is that they sometimes wear headbands and other times blindfolds. It is assumed that this is down to a simple copyist error: in the mid 17th century the blindfold covered the eyes and the heads faced left. In 1952, this representation including the blindfold – with the heads now looking to the right – became the official coat of arms of the island, yet that headband was once again lifted in 1999. Now the moors' heads look to the left again – the official way – and wear a headband.

CORK

Nearly the entire Italian cork production comes from Sardinia, of which the lion's share is harvested in the Gallura region. The bark of a cork oak can only

cially when strangers are present who are not supposed to be part of the conversation. Since 1999, linguists have been creating a standard Sardinian written language as a mix of Sardinian dia-

Originally expressions of political protest, Orgosolo's murales are now a tourist attraction

be peeled off every nine years. After that, the trunks are bright red until a new cork cover has grown back.

LANGUAGE

Donzi populu tenet su derittu a faeddare sa sua limba – every nation has the right to speak their own language. The ruling class has always been hard on the local vernacular. During Spanish rule there was a temporary death penalty imposed for speaking Sardinian. Today most children in rural Sardinia will first learn Sardinian as the mother tongue, picking up Italian only from TV and at school. With strangers they will speak a formal Italian rarely heard on the mainland anymore. Amongst themselves Sardinian is the language of choice, espe-

lects. While it became an official language in 2006, it is hardly used in day-to-day life. Bilingual signs for villages and websites are, however, on the rise.

MURALES

The first impulses came from the Italian student and urban warriors after 1968: politically engaged young artists got to know the murals of Mexico and Chile and adopted the Spanish word *murales*. The subjects came from the Sardinian autonomy movement, increasing protest against the sell-out of the island to the military and tourism companies, but also from Sardinian history, the world of the eternal underdog, the harsh conflicts between landowners and farm hands in the shepherd villages. The slogans in Sardinian are striking and easy to understand. Within a short time, the walls of houses in San Sperate, Serramanna, Villagrande Strisaili, Oliena and Orgosolo became depictions of Sardinia's painful past, in the hope of a better and unconditionally Sardinian future. Laymen have worked alongside professional artists on the *murales*.

There are a large number of nuraghi in the area around Macomer in the north-west

NURAGHI

There are over 8000 of these stone towers in the deserted countryside. Many have only the foundation walls left while others are three storeys tall, with heights of over 12m/40ft. Quite often they form veritable castles, with towers and ring walls several metres thick and form long rows along mountain ridges or on the edges of high plateaus. The nuraghi formed defensive lines, as is easily visible at Macomer and around the Giara di Gesturi. The rock masses and stone blocks, often literally weighing tons, are impressive. The origin of those who built them is unknown, only that they arrived in Sardinia around 1800 BC by sea. Living in several tribal principalities and constantly at war with one another, from around 700 BC onwards, they were first subjugated by the Punic people from Carthage, then by the Romans.

SARACEN TOWERS

Easily distinguished from the nuraghi, these are always right on the coast, and their walls are not as massive. The towers were built between the 15th and 18th century by order of the Spanish viceroys in order to repel attacks by pirates (Saracens), who plundered villages, even those far from the coast, abducting their inhabitants as slaves. 56 towers are still standing, with remains of another 25 still preserved. They probably would have numbered around 100 in total, manned at all times and in constant visual contact with each other.

SHEPHERDS & SHEEP

Shepherds and their flocks are a vital part of the landscape here. With over five million sheep, Sardinia comfortably occupies the top position of the Italian regions. The rough scratchy wool is woven into carpets, blankets and other items in the mountain villages. Lamb meat is in demand and after pecorino cheese brings in the most revenue. Before motors arrived, the shepherds often remained for weeks out on the pasture. The shepherd has to keep the flock healthy as well as make cheese and the curd-like ricotta. And even today, a good part of the cheese is prepared in remote areas rather than in dairies. In winter, the flocks are taken off the mountains into the plains to graze in the maquis or on the fields. Not only the winter grazing has to be paid for, most of the barren mountains pastures too are no longer owned by the community, but are *tancas,* private land enclosed by walls and appropriated in the 19th century when the common ownership was dissolved by edict. Today, young shepherds tend to work with cheese dairies looking after the transport and the processing of the milk. Thanks to carsand roads, they are no longer excluded from having a social life. Their cottages are often still the *pinettas,* the miniature versions of the nuraghi, but now with a TV set and DVD player. With the old shepherds passing on, the picturesque characters wearing velvet suits and tight-fitting peaked caps are now making way for a new generation, which prefers jeans or second-hand outfits from the Italian military surplus stores.

WATER

The issues plaguing Sardinia include forest and maquis fires and month-long droughts that dry up the wells and wither the pastures and fields. In most holiday resorts tourists are little impacted by this but while taps seldom dry, saving water remains an imperative that tourists should also respect. In the towns and many villages in the hinterland, the water only runs for a few hours a day in

Spectacular Cala Luna bay

the summer and autumn. The springs in mountain and forest areas are often besieged by locals with jerrycans and large flasks, because the fresh water tastes better than the tap water, often treated with chlorine.

FOOD & DRINK

Even if pizza and spaghetti feature on the menu, true Sardinian cuisine is very different from that on the Italian mainland. Shepherds, farmers and fishermen all have their own traditions.

Bread beats pasta as Sardinia's main staple. In the pastoral villages of the interior, where many families still do their own baking, the thin crispy flatbread that in its paper-thin round form is called *pane carasau* (the Italians call it *carta di musica* – music paper) and the slightly chunkier rectangular *pane pistoccu*. To make *pane frattau,* a 'Sardinian pizza', this is soaked in water and topped with lamb stew, tomatoes, cheese and poached egg – a dish that's as simple as it is delicious. Pasta too forms an integral part of Sardinian cuisine; spaghetti (originally from mainland Italy) is now very popular. In day-to-day cooking it has now even displaced traditional Sardinian types of pasta like *malloreddus, fregola* or *culurgiones.*

On feast days and Sundays there are often large open air banquets with a fine aroma of suckling pig and lamb wafting through the forests. Hours before it's time to eat the meat is set to spit-roast over hot coals. It's the old men who watch over the roast, and it's their experience that ensures the crispy golden brown crackling and juicy and aromatic meat. Juniper, myrtle and rosemary twigs in the embers lend the smoke its herbal fragrance. However, the true seasonings are the herbs that the animals graze on in the pastures. *A carraxiau* is

Photo: Hotel restaurant Sa Pischedda in Bosa

Suckling pig and hearty red wines, sheep's cheese and bitter honey: the simple, unadulterated cuisine of the Sardinian shepherds and fishermen

the most famous of all the Sardinian specialities, the legendary pit roast. First a huge fire is burnt in a pit in the ground, and then the meat is slow roasted on the embers. This unusual way of preparation probably has its roots in the widespread theft of livestock. When the shepherds wanted to feast on a snatched lamb they would burn a seemingly innocent fire to camouflage the embers in the hole in the ground. The aroma of the pastures – that while sparse are rich in herbs – also goes into the cheese, which ranges in

texture from creamy and soft to rock hard and is mostly made from sheep's milk. The classic *pecorino sardo* is a hard sheep's milk cheese which has matured for at least six months; any older and it is used for grating. An old tradition is the strong-smelling *casu marzu,* where fly larvae turn the hard cheese into a spreadable cream. This is not everybody's cup of tea – it is also banned and not available for sale, as the worms are eaten while still alive. Less adventurous palates will enjoy the variety of mild

LOCAL SPECIALITIES

▶ **acciughe ripiene** – fresh anchovies filled with cheese and breadcrumbs and oven-baked

▶ **agnello al finocchietto selvatico** – lamb stew with fresh wild fennel

▶ **agnello al forno** – lamb braised in the oven with herbs

▶ **bottarga** – dried roe, usually mullet, as a starter or for pasta sauces

▶ **cinghiale** – wild boar

▶ **cordula** – sausages or kebabs made from sheep or goat intestine

▶ **crabiddu** – kid goat

▶ **culurgiones** – pasta pockets with a mixture of vegetables and tomato sauce (photo left)

▶ **fregola** – Sardinian pasta: tiny beads made from durum wheat semolina

▶ **maccarones furriaos** – pasta with cheese curd, a shepherd's dish

▶ **malloreddus** – Sardinian pasta in the shape of small sea shells

▶ **pane guttiau** – Sardinian flatbread with salt and olive oil

▶ **papassinus** – almond pastry with aniseed, cinnamon and cloves

▶ **pardulas** – sweet or savoury pancake turnover

▶ **pasta e fagioli** – thick bean soup with fresh pasta

▶ **porceddu** – spit roast pork suckling, with a crispy crackling

▶ **ravioli di bietola** – pasta pockets filled with ricotta and Swiss chard

▶ **sarde alla marinara** – grilled sardines marinated with oil, lemon and herbs

▶ **se(b)adas con miele amaro** – ravioli filled with ricotta and bitter honey, usually served as a dessert

▶ **torta di ricotta** – sweet ricotta cheese cake

▶ **trattaliu** – skewer of offal with lardons

▶ **zuppa gallurese** – bread soup with a meat broth and grated sheep's milk cheese

▶ **zuppa di pesce** – Sardinian fish soup with tomatoes and toast (photo right)

cheese types such as the *dolce sardo,* a buttery cheese made from cow's milk, the fresh and mild *ricotta*, best from sheep's milk, or the *ricotta salata* with its salty-acidic taste.

Fresh off the boat and roasted on the charcoal grill, sparingly seasoned only with aromatic herbs and a little garlic, fish such as the meaty mullet *(muggine, cefalo)* and even the cheap sardines (sarde) develop an aroma that is only matched by the fishermen's beach picnics. Bees thrive on the flowers of the maquis and wild herbs and their honey is thick and slightly tart – the famous bitter honey is harvested from the *corbezzolo,* or strawberry tree. Eucalyptus and orange blossoms yield a light, viscous and very sweet honey which is used for confectionery and almond pastries.

For decades, Sardinian wine was virtually unknown, as most of the production was for the mass market bottling of 'wines from various EU countries'. This has changed enormously, and now more and more winemakers are working with leading oenologists and are producing quality wines that are causing a stir in wine circles the world over. Every year sees an increase in the number of Sardinian producers whose wines win national and international prizes.

Without a doubt the top Sardinian wine is the red Turriga produced by the Cantina Argiolas from Serdiana, followed closely by the Korem, another red. Other Sardinian tipples that are internationally sought after are the Terre Brune and Rocca Rubia reds from the Cantina of Santadi. The best Cannonau – the classic red wine grape of Sardinia – is made by the Cantina of Oliena, whose Nepente was acclaimed by the iconic Italian writer Gabriele D'Annunzio. A Cannonau newcomer is the boutique winemaker Giuseppe Sedilesu in Mamoiada, who has been winninng the prize race with his Perda Pintà and Mamuthone reds. A rarity is the red Mandrolisai, which is only grown at the foot of the Gennargentu mountain range. Most white wine, and the best – with the Vermentino the most famous here – is cultivated in the Gallura region around Berchidda, Monti and Arzachena. The top tipples from Monti

however are the wonderfully fruity and tangy Funtanaliras and Arakena, the top-ranking wine from Berchidda is the Giogantinu Superiore. The undisputed number one amongst the white wines is, however, ● Capichera, a wine that is as fine as it is expensive, made at the epon-

The dessert wines to go with the Sardinian dolci are produced in the west

ymous *Tenuta di* Capichera (*Mon–Fri 8.30am–1pm and 2.30pm–5pm | www. capichera.it*) near Arzachena. Other well known whites are the light coloured Nuragus from the Campidano and the Aragosta from Alghero. Some superb dessert wines are grown in the west, the Malvasia from Bosa, Sorso and Sennori in particular, as well as the Vernaccia of Oristano, the Sardinian sherry.

SHOPPING

In the Sardinian pastoral villages, many houses still have handlooms where the women use the wool of their sheep to spin carpets and blankets, following ancient patterns. Over the past 40 years, the emigration from the villages and competition from inexpensive modern goods has seen much of the crafts die out. There was no longer a market for pottery, bowls, dishes and jars made from cork, baskets or the wonderful braided items made from asphodel fibres and straw. Then, just in time, the Sardinian Institute for the Promotion of Crafts (I.S.O.L.A) was founded, which provided artisans with premises in the villages, encouraged women to form cooperatives and successfully promoted sales through exhibitions in holiday resorts, in the provincial capitals, in Milan and finally in New York too. Credit must go to I.S.O.L.A. for promoting local crafts especially when you see how, in other places, ancient crafts with centuries-old traditions have disappeared or were displaced by goods produced in low wage countries in Asia or developing countries.

BBQ ACCESSORIES

The numerous markets usually sell a large selection of hand forged skewers, roasting and barbecue racks, fireplace scoops and everything that Sardinians need to grill on an open fire.

CRAFTS

Bowls, jars, plates, chandeliers and ceramics are manufactured following traditional patterns yet with modern designs in the villages of Assemini, Decimomannu, Elmas, San Sperate, Selargius and Serrenti in the Cagliari hinterland. Most of the fine braided items made from natural fibres such as reeds, straw and asphodel plants come from Castelsardo and San Vero Milis, baskets for everyday use can be found on the large markets held with the festivals, in the interior in particular. Carpets and blankets made from wool, linen and cotton are handwoven in Aggius, Osilo, Nule, Bolotana, Dorgali, Fonni, Sarule, Samugheo, Mogoro, San Basilio and Isili. While you're there, take a look at the workshops; choose your pattern, buy and order.

The most authentic souvenirs come from the traditional world of the hardy mountain folk – the shepherds

JEWELLERY

You can find silver and gold filigree work in Alghero, Bosa, Gavoi, Nuoro, Dorgali, Iglesias and Cagliari. You should not buy coral jewellery; while corals used to be found at Alghero and Bosa, these stocks have long been under conservation orders, meaning that the raw material today comes from distant tropical oceans.

KNIVES

If the Sardinians themselves could choose a souvenir from their island, it would probably be a ● traditional shepherd knife from Pattada and Arbus, hand-forged from the best steel, the handle of polished horn chosen for its beauty. A tool – and an art object – that every Sardinian man carries in his pocket.

LEATHER GOODS

Leather belts, often brightly coloured, are an important part of the old costumes and a popular souvenir, as well as the bags and rucksacks made from leather that are manufactured and sold in the mountain villages south of Nuoro.

MUSIC

Sardinia boasts an extraordinarily rich and varied musical scene. Traditional music ranges from the archaic sacred polyphonic *canti sardi* performed by virtuosi players of the *launedda* (a shepherd's flute going back to the Stone Age) such as Cesare Carta, or accordion virtuosi such as the revered Francesco Bande to male choirs such as the famous Tenores di Bitti. Singer-songwriters such as the legendary Maria Carta or modern Sardinian rock bands like the acclaimed Tazenda or Janas use traditional elements, creating a very special and unmistakably Sardinian sound. For a good overview, see *www.zentenoa.com*.

THE PERFECT ROUTE

FROM THE HOLIDAY COAST INTO THE BARBAGIA

Starting from the transport hub of Olbia, drive along the picture-book coastline blessed with many swimming beaches. After taking advantage of these, the route leaves the coast at ① *Orosei* → p. 83 and leads right into the mountains of the Barbagia, the heart and soul of Sardinia. From ② *Orgosolo* → p. 93, the road wends its way uphill and downhill through the sparsely populated mountains. The highlight of this stretch is a summer resort steeped in tradition, ③ *Aritzo* → p. 85 at the foot of Sardinia's highest peak, Punta La Marmora. Beyond Aritzo, the dizzyingly twisting road leads through dense forests of chestnut and fir down into the coastal plain of the Ogliasta and its endless sandy beaches. From Cardedu, the drive leads right into the heart of total isolation. This breathtakingly beautiful stretch runs through a deserted lunar landscape fissured by deep gorges and strewn with imposing rock boulders. At Muravera you once again reach the SS 125 and a quick drive to the top-notch beach of ④ *Costa Rei* → p. 74.

CAGLIARI AND THE BEACHES OF THE SOUTH

A dozen magnificent beaches await at the bustling seaside resort of ⑤ *Villasimius* → p. 74. Don't ignore the capital though, where over a third of the island's population live, as the charming old town of well preserved ⑥ *Cagliari* → p. 59, is still unspoilt by tourism and is easily explored on foot. Your next destination is ⑦ *Santa Margherita di Pula* → p. 65 with the ancient Roman town of Nora.

SARDINIA'S WILD WEST

Now head along the beautiful Costa del Sud into the deserted mining area of Iglesiente. The ancient Phoenicians prospected for ore here. Abandoned mining settlements and ruined mines bear silent witness to that era. With very few roads and devoid of people, the ⑧ *Costa Verde* → p. 68 with its magnificent sandy beaches and dune landscapes is spectacular.

LIGHTNING VISIT TO 'SPANISH' ALGHERO

Via Oristano, our route leads to the ⑨ *Sinis Peninsula* → p. 71 and the ancient Roman town of Tharros at its tip. Picturesque ⑩ *Bosa* → p. 50

Experience the varied facets of Sardinia on this clock-wise drive, with many swim breaks, and spectacular detours into the mountains

nestles on the slope of the palm-fringed Temo; the atmosphere is pleasantly peaceful. To experience the exact opposite, head for neighbouring ⑪ *Alghero* → p. 44: always loud and buzzing, with that typically Mediterranean-chaotic touch and completely un-Italian in aspect because its architecture, language, cuisine and culture are all Spanish-Catalan in influence. The dead straight road leads on to ⑫ *Sassari* → p. 54. Untouched by tourism, the old town is a well preserved maze of narrow streets, ideal for a leisurely stroll (photo above).

THE NORTHERN COAST

The old town of ⑬ *Castelsardo* → p. 52 huddles on a rock that rises steeply above the sea and is crowned by the massive Castello. The stretch of coast that follows is one of the most varied in all of Sardinia. Large parts enjoy protected status and there are signposted hiking trails leading from bay to bay. Park the car and hike along a stretch of the deserted coast! At ⑭ *Capo Testa* → p. 43 with its bizarrely shaped rocks you'll hit the crowds again. ⑮ *Palau* → p. 39 with the La Maddalena coastal national park is a centre for water sports; a day trip by boat, including stops for a dip at some of the most beautiful beaches, makes the trip unforgettable. Finally, the route reaches the legendary ⑯ *Costa Smeralda* → p. 32. While only the select few might be able to afford to take a holiday here, a stroll through Porto Cervo (photo below) is truly an experience! Beyond Porto Cervo, the winding coastal road reveals many splendid vistas of the sea, shimmering in all shades of blue, and its bands of golden beaches.

Distance covered: approx. 1300km/ 800mi. Recommended journey time: at least three to four weeks. Detailed map of the route on the back cover, in the road atlas and the pull-out map.

THE NORTHEAST

Towering granite mountains, high plateaus strewn with boulders as if after a battle of giants, headlands jutting into the sea, and maquis kept short by the wind, the goats and sheep.

The rock – pink, bright white, green, purple – has been polished and shaped by the elements into mythical creatures and animals made from stone: bears, dragons, elephants. When this largely uninhabited coastline was discovered by the Aga Khan, the billionaire fairy-tale prince in 1960, and he proceeded to create a haven for the rich and super-rich in the Costa Smeralda, or Emerald Coast, no tourism existed on the island. Today, the picture-perfect coast between Olbia, Palau and Santa Teresa di Gallura – of which the legendary Costa Smeralda is

but a small part – is Sardinia's most popular holiday region. For a long time now, the wealthy are no longer amongst themselves. The former poorhouse of the island has become its richest asset. Word spread about the granite villages, the prehistoric stone circles, the luminous shimmering green light in the cork oak groves and the expansive horizon. Yet you can walk just a few miles inland and it is infinitely calm and peaceful.

COSTA SMERALDA

(129 E–F 2–4) (*ſ∬* F4–5) **In the early 1960s, the Ismaili Prince Aga Khan –**

Photo: Porto Rotondo marina

Gallura and Costa Smeralda: the barren landscape where Vermentino is produced and not only millionaires enjoy holidaying

himself a keen sailor and a long-time fixture in international high society – 'discovered' the Gallura coast as an ideal sailing area and a new refuge for his circle of friends.

The 22 square miles of coastal maquis, beaches and rocky coves was developed with the help of an international team of architects and landscape planners who created a natural-looking and organically grown holiday landscape. The kinds of harsh interventions into nature found around the Mediterranean were avoided

and only a small part of the available surface was developed. The architects used the traditional fishing villages and farmhouses of the Mediterranean as their model. Natural building materials such as granite and wood were used. The interiors were sparsely furnished with individual pieces of traditional Sardinian and modern arts and crafts. Hotels such as Cala di Volpe, Pitrizza and Romazzino are architectural masterpieces, comparable to the villas of the Renaissance.

The Costa Smeralda and Baia Sardinia

are superb natural landscapes, succeeding in establishing hotels, villas and marinas without destroying or disfiguring the coastline, thanks to the know-how and self-restraint of the architects. However new plans for further expansion are on the cards, which would attract too many visitors, all leaving their mark.

SIGHTSEEING

PORTO CERVO

Porto Cervo is a completely new creation, forming the centre of the Costa Smeral-

FOOD & DRINK

FRATI ROSSI

This small restaurant above the Gulf of Pevero with sea views and Sardinian specialities is located in the Pantogia part of town on the road from Arzachena to Porto Cervo (signposted). *Closed Mon and Oct–March | tel. 0 78 99 43 95 | Moderate–Expensive*

GIAGONI

Enjoy excellent dishes made with produce from the owner's farm, including lamb, ricotta, cheese and vegetables.

The capital of Porto Cervo has typical Costa Smeralda architecture

da. The sailing port has all that the mariner's heart desires, from ship chandlers to dry docks. Porto Cervo has been laid out as a small town, with a church in the typical Costa Smeralda style, with even a real El Greco inside; the Piazza is surrounded by exclusive bars, shops and boutiques. The idea went on to inspire Baia Sardinia and Porto Rotondo.

April–Oct daily | San Pantaleo | Via Zara 43 | tel. 0 78 96 52 05 | Expensive

SHOPPING

Porto Cervo's Piazzetta and the Passeggiata are Sardinia's most select places to shop: jewellery, fashion and Sardinian crafts, as well as antiques can be found at the *Sottopiazza*.

LEISURE, SPORTS & BEACHES

INSIDER TIP DOLPHIN WATCHING

Sardinia's only place to offer unforgettable boat trips to see the dolphins in the La Maddalena national park. The excursions last approx. five hours, depart twice a day in season and cost 100 euros per person. *WWS c/o Orso Diving | Poltu Quatu/Marina dell'Orso | tel. 0 78 99 90 01 | www.whalewatchingsardinia.com*

BEACHES

Pretty as a picture, *La Capriccioli* beach is accessible by car and situated in a sheltered location at the Capriccioli luxury hotel on the peninsula of the same name. At its southern end is *La Celvia,* a gently curved sandy bay. The *Spiaggia Ira* near Porto Rotondo is the favourite beach of European socialite Ira von Fürstenberg. The romantic sandy bay of the *Spiaggia del Principe* extends between rocky cliffs near Romazzino; the *Spiaggia Cala Granu* in a picture-perfect bay on Capo Ferro reached via a footpath (approx. 500m).

WATER SPORTS

Skippers find the necessary gear in Porto Cervo. Popular with windsurfers is the bay of Cannigione and the Golfo di Saline. Boards can be hired at the campsites.

ENTERTAINMENT

On Porto Cervo's Piazzetta as well as on the Piazza in Baia Sardinia, celebrities and their fans come together. Something a bit different is the 'ruined castle' nightclub *Ritual,* built in and on granite rock; its dance floors has long been popular with Costa Smeralda guests.

WHERE TO STAY

INSIDER TIP AGRITURISMO LU BRANU ☆☺

200-year-old organic farm with livestock, honeybees and vineyards – *and* good food. *11 rooms, 5 apartments | along the Arzachena–Palau road 348km/216mi | tel. 0 78 98 30 75 | www.lubranu.it | Budget–Moderate*

CAPRICCIOLI

Small hotel, run by the owner himself, with a fabulous position on the Capriccioli Peninsula. Veranda with restaurant *Pirata,* boat jetty. *46 rooms | tel. 0 78 99 60 04 | www.hotelcapriccioli.it | Expensive*

★ **Archaeological sites**
A sparse rock and moor landscape shelters prehistoric temples and giant tombs → p. 36

★ **Tempio Pausania, Aggius and Monte Limbara**
From the mountain settlement with its pretty old town of pale granite head for the peak, from which on a clear day you can see the entire north of Sardinia → p. 38

★ **Casa Garibaldi**
Built by the Italian national hero himself, today Giuseppe Garibaldi's house on Caprera is an interesting museum → p. 40

★ **Capo Testa**
At the northern tip of Sardinia, immense masses of granite pile up to form impressive sculptures → p. 43

MARCO POLO HIGHLIGHTS

COSTA SMERALDA

INSIDER TIP **CA' LA SOMARA**

Country house in a former donkey stable, handmade carpets and tiles, garden; on request, fine dining too. View of the bay. *12 rooms | Capriccioli | tel. 0 78 99 89 69 | www.calasomara.it | Moderate–Expensive*

ROCCE SARDE ☆

Standing all on its own with beautiful views of the coast. *80 rooms | San Pantaleo | tel. 0 78 96 52 65 | www.roccesarde.com | Expensive*

stone table. 3km/1.8mi from the centre of the town, before you get to the turn for Cannigione, a short footpath to the right leads to the nuraghe of *Albuccio*, built from large granite blocks; right opposite on the road, a footpath leads to the left, which goes along for 1km to the well preserved nuraghe temple of *Malchittu*.

The road to Luogosanto leads to the monumental *Coddu Vecchiu* tomb (look out for signs!) with a large monolith as sepulchral stele. Only 1 km away is the recently excavated nuraghi complex of *La*

An exceptionally well preserved giant tomb is Coddu Vecchiu near Arzachena

WHERE TO GO

ARCHAEOLOGICAL SITES ★
(129 D3) (*⌀ F5*)

Arzachena forms an exception in Gallura, a region otherwise not blessed with many prehistoric monuments. From the centre of town, a narrow road leads to the ☆ *Fungo,* a granite form shaped by wind and rain into a mushroom-shaped

Prisciona. Just under 3km/1.8mi further along towards Luogosanto, a single-track road leads to the monumental tomb of ☆ *Li Lolghi* and the *Li Muri* stone circle, situated in an impressive landscape.

ARZACHENA (129 D3) (*⌀ F5*)

The entire Costa Smeralda (pop. 13,000) occupies the municipality of this once insignificant shepherd's village, as well as Cannigione and Baia Sardinia. The old town centre on the hill with the large Piazza, where the locals meet for the evening *passeggiata*, is not much different from other places with less illustrious surroundings. There has been much construction activity, and signs of prosperity are visible everywhere. However, Arzachena also has some reasonably priced accommodation, and you won't just be amongst tourists.

OLBIA

MAP INSIDE BACK COVER
(129 E5) *(ω F5)* **For most of the holidaymakers travelling to Sardinia by plane or ferry, this port town (pop. 40,000) at the end of a deep bay is their first encounter with the island.**
The architecture that comes into view opposite the granite bastions of the Gallura and the mighty lime slabs of Tavolara Island rarely reaches above two storeys in height.

FOOD & DRINK

GALLURA
Established mid-range hotel *(16 rooms)* in the centre, with a famous gourmet restaurant. Eating here is an experience, because rather than fashionable frills, chef Rita Denza prepares simple but first-rate ingredients to perfection. Rita's cuisine ranks amongst the finest in the whole of Sardinia; reservations definitely required! *Closed Mon | Corso Umberto I 145 | tel. 0 78 92 46 48 | Expensive*

TRATTORIA ROSSI
A few miles east of Olbia on the beach of Pittulongu with views of the island of Tavolara, this trattoria serves seafood with simple anchovies and excellent shellfish. *Closed Wed | tel. 0 78 93 90 42 | www.trattoriarossi.it | Moderate–Expensive*

BEACHES

A municipal bus route goes to *Pittulongu* beach, on the coastal road to Golfo Aranci, which has a lido, restaurants, bars and sports gear for hire. Pretty bays for swimming in the south are *Porto San Paolo, Porto Istana* and *Porto Taverna.*

WHERE TO STAY

SAN PAOLO
Country-house style with garden, running down to the beach bay of the eponymous small harbour 15km/9mi to the south. Superb views of Isola Tavolara. *45 rooms | tel. 0 78 94 00 01 | www.hotel-san-paolo.it | Moderate–Expensive*

INFORMATION

Via Nanni 39 | tel. 07 89 55 77 32 | www.olbiaturismo.it

WHERE TO GO

GOLFO ARANCI AND PORTO ROTONDO (129 F4) *(ω F–G5)*
Golfo Aranci, 15km/9mi north-east, is the second most important ferry port after Olbia. This is where the boats of the Italian state railway from Civitavecchia arrive. The drive from Olbia to here is already pretty (with views over the coast towards the south, and good beaches) and the small fishing harbour, which over the past few years has been prettified into a resort with a seaside promenade and inviting bars and cafés is very inviting.
On the Punta della Volpe Peninsula 15km/9mi to the north, the counterpart to the Costa Smeralda has emerged:

In the land of the cork oaks: the Gallura

Porto Rotondo, with its beautiful hotels and holiday villas, a marina and fine shopping opportunities, attracts a wealthy clientele. At *Giovannino (closed Mon except in summer | tel. 0 78 93 52 80 | Expensive)* on Porto Rotondo's Piazza Quadrata, diners sit in the garden.

INSIDER TIP ▶ OLIVASTRI MILLENARI
(128–129 C–D4) (*M* E–F5)
Tucked away on the northern shore of the Lago di Liscia (access via a cul-de-sac), a true natural wonder awaits: wild olive trees that are thousands of years old. Near the little country church of San Michele are three gigantic wild olive trees next to each other, all of them are healthy and lush. The youngest is well over 1000 years old, the one in the centre has survived for 2500 years, and the awe-inspiring Methuselah, called S'Ozzastru, is an incredible 4000 to 4500 years old: with a trunk diameter of 12m/ 40ft and a mighty crown, it is truly a temple of nature.

TAVOLARA (125 F3) (*M* G5)
This limestone island, 5km/3mi long, rises almost vertically 565m/1853ft out of the sea. When the sea is calm, excursion boats run from Porto San Paolo and Porto Taverna south of Olbia to the small port on the island's western edge, where a few houses line the beach.

TEMPIO PAUSANIA, AGGIUS AND MONTE LIMBARA ★
(128 B–C5) (*M* E5)
Some 35km/22mi west, on the mountains around Calangianus and the ancient capital of the Gallura, Tempio, extends a sparse cork oak forest. Thanks to its location at some 550m/1800ft above sea level Tempio Pausania (pop. 14,000) enjoys a much fresher climate even in summer, which the Sardinians appreci-

ate as much as the cold slightly mineral springs of *Fonti di Rinaggiu* in the upper part of the town. The old town, built from pale granite, is very pretty.

The centrally located *Purgatorio (closed Tue | Via Garibaldi 9 | tel. 0 79 63 40 42 | Budget)* serves local fare with meat, pasta and cheese. 3km/1.8mi outside the town, along the road to Palau, the *Pausania Inn (53 rooms | tel. 0 79 63 40 37 | www.hotelpausaniainn.com | Moderate–Expensive)* has a swimming pool, terrace and a large garden. An exceptionally beautiful place to stay, with a swimming pool and small lake, is the ☺ INSIDERTIP *Agriturismo L'Agnata (12 rooms | tel. 0 79 67 13 84 | www.agnata.it | Moderate–Expensive)* below Monte Limbara on the road to Lago Coghinas. The charming estate, where singer-songwriter Fabrizio De André, fêted as the 'Bob Dylan of Italy', lived up to his death in 1999, is now run as an organic farm by his children.

The peak of the 1359m/4458ft granite massif of 🏔 *Monte Limbara* is accessible by road. On a clear day, views from here take in the entire north of Sardinia all the way to Gennargentu and Corsica. The road from Tempio leads on to the *Lago del Coghinas* with its rich bird life. Tempio's neighbouring village of *Aggius* is famous for its superbly beautiful location below a massive rocky outcrop, its fun-loving inhabitants, and for its traditional weaving. The local *Museo Etnografico Olivia Carta Cannas (Via Monti di Lizu 6 | May–mid Oct daily 10am–1pm and 3pm–7pm)* is not only the largest on Sardinia, it is also the one most worth seeing. Horseback excursions, accommodation and excellent, hearty fare are on offer at the INSIDERTIP *Agriturismo Il Muto di Gallura (10 rooms | Fraiga part of town | tel. 0 79 62 05 59 | www.mutodigallura. com | Budget–Moderate)*.

PALAU AND LA MADDALENA ISLAND

(129 D–E 1–2) *(∅ F4)* **The islands of the Gallurese archipelago are part of a sunken land bridge between Sardinia and Corsica.**

These islands, and the maritime area around them, constitute the *Arcipelago di La Maddalena* national park (for information on access to the protected areas: *Via Giulio Cesare 7 | tel. 07 89 79 02 24 | www. lamaddalenapark.it)*, comprising a good

LOW BUDGET

▶ The bar and pizzeria *Il Baretto (March–Oct daily | tel. 0 78 99 61 15)* on the Costa Smeralda, only a few steps from the famous bay of Cala di Volpe, offers pizzas, snacks and drinks at unexpectedly low prices, considering the area.

▶ A reliable option for particularly cheap and rustic fare is the *Trattoria Cumpai Giuanni (closed Sun | Via dei Lidi | tel. 0 78 95 85 84)* in Olbia.

▶ Visits to both the ● *Museum of Cork Processing (Museo delle Macchine del Sughero | Mon–Fri 8am–2pm, Tue/Wed also 3pm–6pm | Via Limbara 9)* in Tempio Pausania, with displays of 19th century machines and tools, and the new *Archaeological Museum (Mon–Fri 10am–1pm, Mon and Wed also 4pm–6pm)* at Olbia's old port are free of charge.

PALAU AND LA MADDALENA ISLAND

19 square miles on land, 58 square miles of sea surface and a coastline of 112 miles. With its numerous cliffs, shallow waters and stormy coast, this archipelago has always terrified seafarers. Palau (pop. 3900), the access port for La Maddalena, only 15 minutes by boat away, is an active fishing harbour. The magnificent granite formations on Capo d'Orso, the ☼ Monte Altura, crowned by a mighty fortress, and the tall maquis with its substantial biodiversity, as well as some good swimming bays have resulted in holiday resorts similar to the Costa Smeralda.

La Maddalena (pop. 12,000, *www.lama ddalena.com*) has a good natural harbour which was already appreciated by the Romans two millennia ago. Since the end of the 18th century, the hitherto uninhabited island was built up into a fortress. French attempts at conquest failed, including one in 1793, which counted on the participation of a certain Napoleon Bonaparte.

FOOD & DRINK

LA GRITTA ☼
The views from the terrace are breathtaking. Delicious mussels, fish and seafood is served, the desserts are wickedly tempting and there is also always a fine selection of cheeses. *Daily | Porto Faro north of Palau | tel. 07 89 70 80 45 | Expensive*

SU SIRBONE ☼
A little outside Palau its situation on a hill means that there are fabulous views across the islands, the cooking references more the traditions of the interior. *May–Sept daily | tel. 07 89 70 84 48 | Moderate–Expensive*

LA TERRAZZA
Above the old town with views of the harbour, enjoy fried sea anemones, pasta with seafood and fresh fish. *Closed Sun | La Maddalena | Via Villa Glori 6 | tel. 07 89 73 53 05 | Moderate*

SPORTS

Porto Puddu, 8km/5mi north-west of Palau, is considered one of the island's best windsurfing spots; access is via the holiday resort of Barrabisa.

WHERE TO STAY

NIDO D'AQUILA
Great location on the coastal road leading north. *38 rooms | La Maddalena | tel. 07 89 72 21 30 | www.hotelnidodaquila.it | Moderate*

HOTEL LA VECCHIA FONTE
New hotel with fine views on to Palau's marina. Bright, spacious rooms. *36 rooms | Via Fonte Vecchia 48 | tel. 07 89 70 97 50 | www.lavecchiafontehotel. it | Moderate–Expensive*

INFORMATION

La Maddalena | Piazza Barone Des Geneys | tel. 07 89 73 63 21 | www.lama ddalena.com; Palau | Palazzo Fresi | tel. 07 89 70 70 25 | www.palau.it

WHERE TO GO

CAPO D'ORSO ☼ (129 E2) (𝄢 F4)
A scenic road (4km/2.5mi) above the coast with wonderful vistas of the archipelago. Occupying a prominent position above the cape is the 'bear', a colossal granite rock in the shape of a bear, is accessed by a 500m path *(admission 2 euros)* leading uphill.

CASA GARIBALDI ★ (129 E2) (𝄢 F4)
While La Maddalena is fairly barren and rocky, with only some small coves, the

island of Caprera (they are connected by a causeway) is forested, and has sandy and pebbly coves in its southern part. The Italian national hero, Giuseppe Garibaldi, settled on Caprera in 1861, having started his conquest of Sicily and south-

tower, *Budelli* has pink sand and *Razzoli* is rugged. Some islands (and parts of islands) form part of the main zone of the national park and are off limits – one of them is the famous pink coral beach of Budelli, which had to close because visi-

By boat through the Gallurese archipelago

ern Italy with his 1000 redshirts from here. After the unification of Italy, Garibaldi built the Casa Bianca himself, cultivated the land und received countless admirers. After his death in 1882, he was buried in the garden beneath a huge piece of granite. Today, his house is a museum and national memorial. *Caprera Island | Tue–Sun 9am–6.30pm | www.compendiogaribaldino.it*

tors carried the sand off in bags. Any interference with nature – whether underwater hunting, fishing or a barbecue on the beach – is strictly prohibited.

SANTA TERESA DI GALLURA

ISLAND TRIPS ● (129 D1) (∅ F4)
Daily trips to the smaller islands are on offer in Palau and La Maddalena, with or without meals on board, but usually with a stop for a swim. The largest is *Spargi* with a few stone huts and a Saracen

(128 C1) (∅ E4) **Only 12km/7.5mi of sea separate Corsica and Sardinia and ferries from Santa Teresa di Gallura commute several times a day to Bonifacio. As you arrive Bonifacio forms a backdrop to the high forested mountains of**

southern Corsica, its white cliffs shining luminously on clear days.

Santa Teresa (pop. 4200) is a fishing port. While opportunities for swimming

na Island. *Cala Sambuco* and *La Marmorata* are two superb beaches right next to the other; swimmers can easily explore the off-shore Marmorata islets with

Erosion has shaped the granite rocks at Capo Testa into bizarre formations

here are limited, there are glorious bathing beaches in the surroundings such as at Capo Testa.

FOOD & DRINK

S'ANDIRA ☀☾

On the beach at Santa Reparata with fabulous views of the sea and Corsica, served up with fish, seafood and sushi. *May–Oct daily | Via Orsa Minore 1 | tel. 07 89 75 42 73 | Expensive*

BEACHES

The town's main beach of *Rena Bianca* is a fine sandy bay right below the town. On the *Spiaggia Valle d'Erica,* a long sandy bay with individual small pebbly coves between mighty granite boulders, you can swim with a view of La Maddale-

the ruins of an old Roman grotto. The beautiful, long sandy beach of *Rena Maiore,* with dunes and shady pine trees, is 8km/5mi outside the town near the SP 90 to Vignola Mare.

WHERE TO STAY

CORALLARO

Right on the sandy beach of Rena Bianca, with large rooms and a swimming pool. *82 rooms | tel. 07 89 75 54 75 | www.ho telcorallaro.it | Moderate–Expensive*

AGRITURISMO SALTARA ☀☾ ☺

Organic livestock farming, with a loft and five bungalows in the park, as well as a restaurant. 2km/1.2mi from Rena Maiore beach in Li Pinneti. *Tel. 07 89 75 55 97 | www.agriturismosaltara.it | Budget–Moderate*

INSIDER TIP AGRITURISMO SOLE E TER-RA ☺

Located 20km/12mi to the south, near Bassacutena, this biodynamic farm is far off the road in the peaceful countryside and has its own stream. It offers excellent cuisine (also vegetarian dishes!), cookery classes, a swimming pool, horse riding and a cycle centre (www.gallurabikepoint. com/eng/) offering both mountain bike and racing bike tours for beginners and professionals. *6 rooms | Funtana d'Alzu part of town | tel. 33 15 84 69 91 | www. soleeterra.it | Budget–Moderate*

INFORMATION

Piazza Vittorio Emanuele 24 | tel. 07 89 75 41 27 | www.comunestg.it

WHERE TO GO

CAPO TESTA ★ ● (128 B1) (*E4*)
The granite masses of the nearby peninsula of Capo Testa are an experience – there are stone formations in the shape of animals, castles and mythical creatures and the really spectacular ones are in the 'moon valley' **INSIDER TIP** *Valle di Luna*.

SAN TEODORO AND BUDONI

(125 F3–4) (*G6*) **With its widely curving granite and sandy bays and small shepherd hamlets in the hinterland, the south of the Gallura region is reminiscent of the island's mountainous interior.**
Over the course of 30 years, clusters of houses and shepherd huts have grown into holiday resorts and proper villages. There are hardly any major hotels; instead accommodation is in holiday villages, apartments and campsites.

San Teodoro (pop. 1700) has long wide beaches – a 3km/1.8mi long sandy strip *La Cinta* divides the lagoon from the sea and offers the perfect beach experience. In the north there are cliffs where divers find spots full of marine life, such as at Lu Impostu and Capo Coda Cavallo. The *Museo del Mare (Mon–Fri 10am–1pm and 4.30pm–7pm)* with aquarium, lies on the access road to the main La Cinta beach. In a fabulous location on the Punta Aldia Peninsula north of San Teodoro is the *Due Lune (67 rooms | tel. 07 84 86 40 75 | www.duelune.com | Expensive)*. A fine choice indeed – thermal baths, golf course, spa complex – set in gardens stretching down all the way to the sea. Information: *Piazza Mediterraneo | tel. 07 84 86 57 67 | www.santeodoro turismo.com).Budoni (information: Via Nazionale 202 | tel. 07 84 84 40 50 | www. prolocobudoni.it)*, a village extending along a single street, boasts long picture-perfect beaches with magnificent pine groves and powdery sand. The two nearby hamlets of *Agrustos* and *Ottiolu* have preserved their rural charm.

WHERE TO GO

ALTOPIANO DI BUDDUSÒ
(125 D–E4) (*E–F 6–7*)
From the shepherd's village of *Alà dei Sardi* (a good 50km/31mi from Budoni), a signposted dirt road leads after 8km/5mi to the nuraghe sanctuary of *sos Nurattolos*, with well preserved temples and well sanctuaries. Beyond *Buddusò*, the road leads through cork oak groves in the direction of Bitti; taking in the impressive *Nuraghe Loelle* along the way. A side road leads to the prehistoric *su Romanzesu* (well temple, megalithic circles). The fame of the excellent traditional cooking at *Agriturismo Ertila (daily | tel. 07 84 41 45 58 | www.agriturismoertila.it | Budget)* has spread throughout the entire region, despite its isolated location near the road from Bitti to Mamone.

THE NORTHWEST

The trees stand tall like flagpoles, slightly askew, showing the way the wind blows. The maestrale, as Italian seafarers call the mistral coming in from the south of France, hits land again here after 350km/220mi at sea, drying out the soil where no mountains or even field walls, offer protection.

Porto Torres and Stintino are protected from the wind by the island of Asinara, and Alghero by the hills of Capo Caccia. Those are the few quiets corners and the only ports of any importance. The largest part of the coast is deserted and inaccessible from the land. Porto Torres, today disfigured by petrochemical industrial plants, has been the end point of the great Sardinian north-south road since Roman times and as such, the springboard to northern Italy. The villages of the high plains are a significant distance from the coast. The past wealth of shepherds and horse breeders is illustrated by the nuraghi constructions from prehistory and the Romanesque and Pisan churches of the High Middle Ages, which today seem huge amongst the villages, shrunk to only a few houses.

ALGHERO

(130 A1) (*ØØ B–C7*) **The most magnificent vista of Alghero (pop. 44,000) is from the south, from the coastal road to Bosa.**

This particular perspective hides the part of the new town that has concrete high-

Photo: Capo Caccia at Alghero

Coastal towns, sea caves and extinct volcanoes: the northwest is one of the most popular Sardinian holiday destinations

rises, half of them hotels, displaying instead the peninsula with the old town and its ring of imposing defensive towers, the slender church towers and colourfully glazed ceramic domes. The wide bay beyond provides a spectacular setting for Capo Caccia with its white chalk rocks in the distance. Both are connected by the deep green Pineta and a long snowwhite sandy beach.

In 1355 Spanish troops conquered the city after a long siege. The few survivors were deported to the Balearics as slaves. The Catalans enjoyed privileges and turned Alguer into the most important port and trading hub in Sardinia after Cagliari. The mighty bastions protected against attack from the sea and were never conquered. The right to expel all non-Catalans from the city at night protected against infiltration by land.

Today the city centre is still in Catalan hands, from the bakeries to the goldsmiths and coral cutters. The jade jewellery and corals for sale are from East Asia,

The Catalan past is still present in the lanes of Alghero

SIGHTSEEING

OLD TOWN ★

Entering the town through one of the city gates it quickly becomes apparent that Alghero is different. The street signs are bilingual, their names – Calle Mallorca and Calle Barcelona – testimonies to its Spanish-Catalan past. The Catalan language is still alive in the alleyways while the façades and beautifully wreathed stone details around windows and gates, and the heavy vaults, the churches and palaces are in the Gothic style of northern Spain. The most impressive are the cloisters and church of *San Francesco* – an oasis of quiet in the heart of the old town. Also worth seeing is the *Palazzo Machin*.

FOOD & DRINK

MACHIAVELLO

Welcoming osteria right on the bastion with fine cuisine. But the truly splendid feature is the ☘ terrace overlooking the city with fabulous views, especially at sunset. *Closed Tue | Bastioni Marco Polo 57 | tel. 0 79 98 06 28 | www.osteriamac chiavello.it | Moderate*

AL TUGURI

Well established gourmet restaurant with creative local cuisine and some illustrious guests. The dining room is small so it is a good idea to make a reservation. Appropriate dress is required. *Closed Sun | Via Maiorca 113 | tel. 0 79 97 67 72 | Moderate–Expensive*

SHOPPING

A large variety of gold and silver jewellery can be found all over the old town. Souvenir suggestions are the olive oils of the ☺ *Accademia Olearia,* which have

as the coral grounds of Alghero and Bosa have long since been exhausted. A INSIDER TIP▶ stroll through the bastions with a view of the harbour and Capo Caccia, aimless ambling on the ancient cobbles, their stone paving polished smooth, will give you a better idea of Alghero than dutifully traipsing around its rather uninteresting churches, with the exception of San Francesco.

won several awards and include an excellent organic variety. Unique is the *Casa del Pane (Via Manzoni 78),* where you'll find all manner of tasty breads and pastries, and sweet-toothed visitors will be in heaven at *Bons Bons (Via Einaudi 21),* which sells handmade sweet temptations made in the traditional Catalan confectionery style. Crafts are for sale at *Marogna (Piazza Civica 34),* and a goldsmith bridging modern and traditional styles is *Rosanna Scala (Via Sassari 182).* The *market hall* is in *Via Sassari.* Conservation concerns and their provenance – East Asia! – should stop anyone from buying the coral jewellery for sale in many places.

SPORTS & BEACHES

BOAT TRIPS AND CRUISES

Excursions to the Grotta di Nettuno and round trips, some with glass bottom boat, start at the harbour.

LIDO SAN GIOVANNI

The beach of San Giovanni, near a pine grove with fine sand next a lido with sun lounger and sunshade hire, offers 5 km/3mi of beach with plenty of room. On the municipal bus route.

ENTERTAINMENT

Most of the action happens in the old town, in the bars and ice-cream parlours on the *Piazza Sulis* and Lungomare Colombo up to Torre San Giacomo.

WHERE TO STAY

RIVIERA

Near the old town, and not far from the sandy beach and the shore promenade, this holiday hotel is run by the owners themselves. *55 rooms | Via Fratelli Cervi 6 | tel. 0 79 95 12 30 | www.hotelriviera-alghero.com | Moderate–Expensive*

INSIDER TIP SAN FRANCESCO

In the heart of the old town above the cloisters of the eponymous monastery. Simple, quiet rooms adequately furnished. Book in advance! *20 rooms | Via Machin 2 | tel. 0 79 98 03 30 | www.san francescohotel.com | Moderate*

VILLA LAS TRONAS

Once the luxury summer villa of the Italian royal family, today it is an exclusive five star hotel in a stunning location right by the sea. With spa. *25 rooms | Lungomare Valencia 1 | tel. 0 79 98 18 18 | www.hotelvillalastronas. it | Expensive*

INFORMATION

Piazza Porta Terra 9 | tel. 0 79 97 90 54 | www.alghero-turismo.it

---

MARCO POLO HIGHLIGHTS

★ **Alghero old town**
The city is strongly influenced by its Catalan past → p. 46

★ **Asinara Island**
National park with wild, white donkeys and untouched nature → p. 49

★ **Bosa old town**
Cobbled alleyways and houses built from pink stone – a small-town idyll → p. 50

★ **San Pietro di Sorres**
Monastery church erected in the 12th century by Tuscan master builders → p. 56

WHERE TO GO

CAPO CACCIA AND GROTTA DI NETTUNO (124 A4) (*00 B7*)

Beyond Fertilia, the coast changes character, dramatic limestone mountains drop right down to the shoreline, rising softly at first, then turning into a sheer rock face at Capo Caccia, jutting up vertically hundreds of feet from the sea. Narrow roads lead to the beach coves and holiday villages of *Spiaggia Bombarde, Lazzaretto* and *Maristella,* where you'll also find the major hotels.

The nuraghi complex of *Palmavera* is not only unusual for its location, just under 10km/6mi north-west right on the coast, but also for the very careful way the stone has been worked. The complex had a strong ring wall and a central edifice with two towers. The round hut at the entrance probably served for counsel sessions, as suggested by a throne of sandstone and the stone bench running around it. The deep bay of *Porto Conte*, protected as a nature park, is one of the best natural ports in the Mediterranean; the road is lined by pine groves, and much of the beach is accessible.

On its way to the lighthouse 25km/15mi west on *Capo Caccia*, the road rises

Those not too keen on the idea of 652 steps can also go to the Grotta di Nettuno from Alghero by boat

and then ends above the *Grotta di Nettuno (May–Sept daily 9am–7pm, April and Oct 9am–6pm, Nov–March 10am–3pm),* which is reached by the Escala de Cabriol stepped pathway, leading down 200m/656ft on 652 steps. The view from the cape on to Alghero and the coast in the direction of Bosa is overwhelming. 2km/1.2mi before the cave, running across the back of the cape, a trail forks off through the wind-blown maquis to the northern coast. Also accessible from Alghero and Porto Conte by boat, the cave is one the most beautiful (and largest) sea grottoes in Italy. Guided tours through the fairy-tale world of stalactites, lakes and large caverns take place hourly.

NECROPOLIS OF ANGHELU RUJU
(124 A4) *(ш B6)*

With its 37 burial caves from the Ozieri culture (3400–2700 BC) and the subsequent Bonnanaro culture, this necropolis is one of the largest and most important in the Mediterranean. It is situated on the grounds of the famous *Sella & Mosca* vineyard *(www.sellaemosca.it)*, which also produces an exquisite heavy liqueur wine called Anghelu Ruju. *April–Oct daily 9am–7pm, March 9.30am–4pm, Nov–Feb 10am–2pm*

INSIDER TIP **PORTO FERRO, ARGENTIERA, STINTINO AND ASINARA**
North of Porto Conte and Capo Caccia there are even more sandy beaches with dunes and dwarf palms (which only occur here and on the Sinis Peninsula) then up to the north-western point at the Capo del Falcone the coast becomes steep and practically inaccessible even from the sea. Beyond *Torre del Porticciolo* and *Porto Ferro* (124 A4) *(ш B6)* there are only narrow dead-end roads, while between the two bays your only companions will be dunes, cliffs and solitude.

Through reclaimed swamp lands and then on a rough road through the barren hills of the Nurra, head via the hamlet of Palmadula to the abandoned silver mines of *Argentiera* (124 A4) *(ш B6)* 35km/22mi north. In the 19th century a true silver rush took place, after an improved smelting technique made the slag heaps – left behind by the Romans and the Punics – yield the coveted metal. Most prospectors didn't make any money at all or even get their chance to try their luck, such as French novelist Honoré

de Balzac back in 1838. Depending on the swell, the small beach around the derelict lading port has some good diving.

Not until just before Stintino, does the road changes to the gentle eastern side of the peninsula. The former salt ponds and the buildings of the Tonnara, where tuna used to be slaughtered and preserved, are today a modern sailing sports centre. *Stintino* (124 A3) *(ш B5)*, 60km/37mi, to the north, curves around a small harbour bay and, outside of high season, is a quiet fishing village with colourful houses, small gardens and tree-lined streets. Accommodation and sustenance may be found in the renovated hotel *Geranio Rosso (15 rooms | Via XXI Aprile 8 | tel. 079 52 32 92 | Budget–Moderate)*, where the chef prepares whatever fresh fish the boats bring in. The main attraction of Stintino is the famous *Spiaggia Pelosa* at Capo del Falcone, around which holiday resorts have spread out. Blessed with incredible colours, this beach is often used for advertising and fashion shoots.

Up to 1884 only fishermen and shepherds lived on ★ *Asinara Island* (124 A2) *(ш B5)*. Now a national park, the island was a penal colony between 1896 and 1998, a feared high-security prison, Italy's own Alcatraz. Special not only for its pristine nature, idyllic coves for swimming and the sombre remains of the prison, Asinara is also home to the famous wild, white donkeys, whose origin is unknown. Inexpensive accommodation is on offer at the simple *Sognasinara guest house (28 beds in 1 to 8-bed rooms | tel. 34 61 73 72 19 | www.sognasinara.org | Budget)*, housed in a restored prison building in Cala d'Oliva. Asinara can be visited from Stintino and Porto Torres either independently or as part of a guided tour on foot, bicycle, horseback, bus or electric train.

Information and reservations under *www. parcoasinara.org*.

BOSA

(130 B4) (*M C8*) **The small town (pop. 7800) lies 4km/2.5 inland in the Temo river valley. The river is navigable (the only one in Sardina) for small boats up to the bridge at the upper town gate op-** posite the cathedral.

A palm-fringed promenade leads along the Temo riverbank. Opposite are the abandoned tanneries of *sas Conzas*. A quiet rural atmosphere reigns in the streets and squares with their old pebble stone pavements, in the weathered palaces and narrow lanes of the ★ old town, almost entirely built out of the local pink trachyte stone. Women sit with their embroidery at their front door while the men are more attracted to the dark vaults where the famous Malvasia wine is served, or the old-fashioned and sparsely furnished bars.

SIGHTSEEING

CASTELLO DEI MALASPINA ☆
A stepped path leads through the old town to the castle, with its defensive wall and towers, erected by the Genovese. *April–June daily 10am–1pm and 3.30pm–6.30pm, July/Aug 10am–1pm and 4pm–7.30pm, Sept/Oct 10am–1pm and 3.30pm–6pm, Nov–March Sat/Sun 10am–1pm*

SAN PIETRO EXTRAMUROS
From the Temo bridge, along the bank facing away from the town, a street leads through gardens in full bloom to the Romanesque church (30 min on foot), erected between the 11th and 13th centuries by Burgundian builders.

FOOD & DRINK

MANNU
Neither the location nor the simply furnished dining room would suggest that this place serves the best food in Bosa, and at very fair prices, which is why you'll meet a lot of locals here too. Try the *risotto al pescatore* – a dream! *Daily | Viale Alghero 14 | tel. 07 85 37 53 07 | www. mannuhotel.it | Moderate*

RICCARDO

In this inconspicuous trattoria (10km/6mi south in the village of Magomadas) the amateur fisherman and Slow Food aficionado Riccardo serves mouthwatering cuisine – the fish and seafood caught by the man himself are worth trying, but the meat dishes and the mushrooms are excellent too. Definitely book ahead! *Closed Tue | Magomadas | Via Vittorio Emanuele | tel. 0 78 53 56 31 | Budget*

INSIDER TIP ZIA GIOVANNA

Located in Padria (25 km/15mi away) behind the Romanesque church: old fashioned and a bit cramped, welcoming atmosphere. There is no menu, the food changes daily, using seasonal products. *Closed Sat | Padria | Via Fratelli Sulis 9 | tel. 0 79 80 70 74 | Budget*

SHOPPING

Goldsmithing has a long tradition in Bosa. Beautifully crafted pieces can be purchased from *Antonio Sotgiu (Viale della Repubblica 14)* and at *Vadilonga (Corso Vittorio Emanuele 48)*.

SPORTS & BEACHES

The beach of the marina – often very full – and Turas beach further south both have dark yellow sand. There are excellent diving opportunities along the coastal road to Alghero at the *Torre Argentina* on the rocky coast with its bizarre formations and bright colours; though even a low swell makes diving here risky. From the farming village of Tresnuraghes to the south, a road leads for 11km/7mi across the barren plateau the INSIDER TIP *Punta di Foghe,* where an isolated beach cove awaits at the end of a long gorge.

View of the idyllic Bosa on the Temo

GRIFFON VULTURE WATCHING

One of INSIDER TIP Europe's last remaining griffon vulture colonies nests in the rugged cliffs at Capo Marargiu north of Bosa. Those who would like to take a closer look at these giants of the sky with their wing span of up to 2.8m/9ft can take part in one of the expertly guided excursions. Information and booking: *Saverio Biddau (tel. 0 34 77 69 13 33) or Antonello Cossu (tel. 0 34 75 48 27 18)*

WHERE TO STAY

INSIDER TIP CORTE FIORITA

Two stylishly expanded houses in the old town with 30 rooms and holiday apartments, the ☆ main house overlooks the river. *Lungotemo 45 | tel. 07 85 37 70 58 | www.albergo-diffuso.it | Budget–Moderate*

SA PISCHEDDA

A small, simple house on the Temo with a history going back over 100 years. Restaurant with garden and creative seafood fare *(in winter closed Tue | Moderate)*. *7 rooms | Via Roma 8 | tel. 0785373065 | www.hotelsapischedda. it | Budget–Moderate*

INFORMATION

Via Azuni 5 | tel. 078537 6107 | www. infobosa.it

WHERE TO GO

MACOMER (131 D4) *(ⓜ D8)*

Situated 35km/22mi to the east, Macomer (pop. 11,000) is surrounded by a ring of nuraghi, clearly visible along the road. Worth a vist are the nuraghe of ⚘ *Santa Barbara* on the ring road (car park), and the *Zona Archeologica di Tamuli (June–Sept Tue–Sun 10am–1pm and 3pm–7pm, Oct–May Fri–Sun 10am–1pm or by request | tel. 0785746034)* near the road to Santu Lussurgiu. Particularly impressive are the *Sei Betili,* six mysterious conical menhirs facing each other in two rows, three of which have breast-like protuberances.

SANTA SABINA (131 E4) *(ⓜ D8)*

The way Christianity used ancient sanctuaries for the new faith can be seen in this small Byzantine country church some 50km/31mi east of Silanus right next to a nuraghe.

IL TRENINO VERDE

⚘ (130 B4) *(ⓜ C8)*

Departing from Bosa Marina, the narrow gauge railway train runs to Macomer via Tresnuraghes. The scenic route has many hairpin bends and fabulous views. The little train only runs from mid June to mid September, on Fridays and Sundays at 9.30am from Macomer and at 4.30pm from Bosa Marina. Information and tickets: *Trenino Verde Point Bosa | Coop Esedra | Corso Vittorio Emanule 64 | tel. 0785374258 | www.esedrasardegna. it*

CASTELSARDO

(124 C3) *(ⓜ D5)* **This small coastal town (pop. 5200) with its Genovese castle of a Rocca and its distinctive church tower, with glazed tile dome, occupies a huge rock right above the sea.**

Narrow lanes and stepped paths make the old town a pedestrian reserve, here the old people like to sit outside their front door, the women embroidering or weaving bowls out of colourful raffia. The romantic scenery has turned Castelsardo into a very popular tourist resort, even though the beaches near the town are small, bare and stony.

SIGHTSEEING

CATHEDRAL SANT'ANTONIO ABATE

The cathedral has a High Gothic interior. The winged altar executed by the 'Maestro of Castelsardo' dates from the 15th century.

FOOD & DRINK

CORMORANO

Fish and seafood – the menu offers whatever is caught on the day. *Daily | Via Colombo 5 | tel. 0794706 28 | Moderate–Expensive*

DA UGO

Refined seafood delicacies on the beach of Lu Bagnu, in a quiet family ambience, complemented by an excellent wine list. Prices are fair given the outstanding quality. Particularly delicious are the super-fresh *antipasti al mare*. *Closed Thu | Corso Italia 7 c | tel. 07 89 47 41 24 | www. ristorantedaugo.eu | Moderate*

BEACHES

The endless beaches of Valledoria and Badesi offer fabulous opportunities for swimming. Windsurfing boards can be

INFORMATION

Piazza del Popolo 1 | tel. 0 79 47 15 06

WHERE TO GO

ANGLONA (124 C3) (*m D5–6*)

Beyond the coast marks the start of the rather unspectacular mountain country of Anglona, bare, with extensive plains, small villages, a few pretty country churches – a drive off the beaten track.

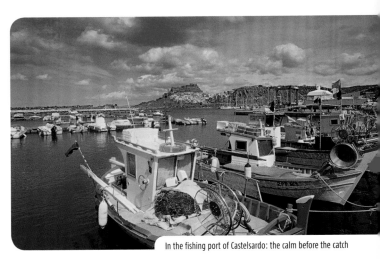

In the fishing port of Castelsardo: the calm before the catch

hired through the campsites in Valledoria. The beaches of Marina di Sorso and Platamona are flat with sand and pine forests, ideal for children.

WHERE TO STAY

NADIR ❄️

In a panoramic location above the steep coast. *32 rooms | Via Colle di Frigiano 1 | tel. 0 79 47 02 97 | www.hotelnadir.it | Moderate–Expensive*

Right at the beginning of the road leading inland to Sedini is the famous Roccia dell'Elefante *of Castelsardo,* a weathered trachyte rock shaped like an elephant. The cavity inside is a prehistoric *domus de janas* burial site. The village of *Sedini,* a good 15km/9mi to the south-east, boasts houses built into *domus de janas.* A little further on, beyond Bulzi, a road turns off east to the isolated Pisan church of *San Pietro di Simbranos,* with black and white zebra-style inlays. From Martis, a dirt track leads to the petrified forest in the *Parco Paleobotanico.*

SASSARI

MAP INSIDE BACK COVER
(124 B4) (*ⁿ* C6) **Following the fall of the Roman Empire, the ancient port town of Turris (today Porto Torres) was abandoned by its inhabitants due to the unsafe coasts and malaria. Instead, they founded the new inland town of Sassari.**

Sassari (pop 130,000) was always a vibrant trading hub that enjoyed freedoms and privileges, even in times of the worst feudal rule, such as under the Spanish viceroys.

The first impression of Sassari is that of a modern, clean and obviously wealthy town. The completely intact old town, which had become uninhabited over the past decades, is being revitalised. With its narrow lanes, many not accessible by car, and its light-coloured houses and small squares it is often more reminiscent of a village. The Corso Vittorio Emanuele II, the town's main shopping and pedestrian street, begins near the railway station and ends at the Piazza d'Italia, where the 19th century state showed its presence with vast administrative buildings.

SIGHTSEEING

CATHEDRAL
Built during the 14th century in Catalan Gothic style, which has been preserved inside, the cathedral's façade was redesigned in the 17th and 18th centuries in highly ornamental Spanish colonial baroque.

MUSEO NAZIONALE SANNA
Of particular interest here is the archaeological department, housing finds from all periods of Sardinian prehistory and early history, including small bronzes, menhirs (tall upright stones) and weapons. *Via Roma 64 | Tue–Sun 9am–8pm | www.museosannasassari.it*

INSIDER TIP MUSEO FRANCESCO BANDE ●
The collection of the Sardinian folk musician Francesco Bande (1930–88) shows musical instruments and costumes from his hometown of Bultei. *Via Muroni 44 | Mon–Fri 10am–noon | www.museobande.com*

SAN PIETRO DI SILKI
The interior of this very popular pilgrimage church on the outskirts of town displays a harmonious juxtaposition of simple Romanesque medieval and ceremonious baroque. *1.5km/1mi in the direction of the SS 131*

SANTA MARIA DI BETLEM
Once situated outside the city, today's church is reminiscent of a mosque due to its dome and slender round tower. The Romanesque façade is still well preserved. Inside are the nine colourful huge wooden candles decorated with tinsel that are ceremoniously carried through the streets of the city during the procession of the city's guilds on 14 August – the eve of Ascension Day.

FOOD & DRINK

SA PEDRA NUDA
A young kitchen team in the old town, which also dares to attempts vegetarian fare (rare in Sardinia) and there is also lot of seafood on the menu. *Closed Sun | Via Eleonora d'Arborea 13 | tel. 0 79 23 87 99 | Moderate*

LA VELA LATINA
The reasonably priced trattoria in the old town has stayed true to the hearty fare

enjoyed by regular Sardinians. *Closed Sun | Largo Sisini 3 | tel. 079 23 37 37 | Budget–Moderate*

SHOPPING

PALAZZO DELL'ARTIGIANATO
The pavilion in the city park displays the entire range of Sardinian crafts to browse and buy. *Viale Mancini*

WHERE TO STAY

BED & BREAKFAST CASA CHIARA
Three generous guest rooms in a historic palazzo in Sassari's old town near Piazza Azuni. *Vicolo Bertolinis 7 | tel. 07 92 00 50 52 | www.casachiara.net | Budget*

HOTEL VITTORIO EMANUELE
Well established classic city hotel with 45 rooms in the centre. *Corso Vittorio Emanuele 100–102 | tel. 079 23 55 38 | www.hotelvesassari.it | Moderate*

INFORMATION

Via Sebastiano Satta 13 | tel. 07 92 00 80 72 | www.comune.sassari.it

WHERE TO GO

RIDING THE NARROW GAUGE TRAIN TO TEMPIO ●
(124–125 B–D3) (C–E 5–6)
A scenic rail trip with many hairpin bends and only a few miles into the two hour journey, you'll see expanse and solitude, nuraghi, country churches and stunning mountain views. The landscape changes beyond the bridge over the Coghinas. Red granite masses start rising up, alternating with dark green maquis. *Mid June–mid Sept Fri 9am from Sassari, 5pm from Tempio (the narrow gauge all year round on the Sassari–Alghero, Sassari–Sorso and Sassari–Nulvi lines) | www.treninoverde.com*

Pisan Romanesque style: façade of the Santissima Trinità di Saccargia in Logudoro

LOGUDORO

In the Middle Ages, the Logudoro and the table mountains of the Meilogu supplied horses to the city republics of central Italy. This tradition has survived in the two state-owned stud farms of Chilivani and Foresta di Burgos, where racehorses are bred. Along the road to Olbia, the church of INSIDER TIP *Santissima Trinità di Saccargia* (124 C4) (D6) is visible from afar. The ornate façade and the portico count amongst the masterpieces of Pisan architecture. The stone inlay of the gable and the animal capitals and friezes of the portal arches in particular, as well as the slender tower, are remarkable. On the edge of the nearby small village of *Codrongianos*, an old

tarpiece, which fills the entire height and breadth of the room and radiates its gold and colours into the dark space.

Ittireddu (131 E1) *(ɱ D7)* is one of the small shepherd's villages on the edge of the *Valle dei Nuraghi*. There are very few other parts of the island where prehistoric sites cluster so densely. The town

Trachyte sculpture in the necropolis of Sant'Andria Priu at Bonorva in Logudoro

manor house, surrounded by a park and orchard, has been turned into a hotel: *Hotel Funtanarena | 9 rooms | tel. 0 79 43 50 48 | www.funtanarena.it | Moderate.*

⚜ *Ardara* (124 C4) *(ɱ D6)* is situated some 30km/18mi south-east on a hilltop with expansive views over the Logudoro plain. The small village is dominated by the 'black cathedral' of *Santa Maria del Regno*, the coronation church of the Sardinian kings during the time of the giudicati. It was erected in 1107 by Tuscan master builders. Thick columns with bulky leaf capitals divide the three naves. On entering, the eye is drawn straight away to the 16th century INSIDER TIP al-

hall houses a remarkable *Museum of Prehistory and Folk Culture (Sun–Fri 10am–1pm and 3pm–6pm)*. The costumes, carpets, blankets, work tools and household items date from the most recent past and the present. Signposted archaeological walks in the surrounding area lead to *domus de janas,* wells, chamber tombs and nuraghi. On the street leading from Mores to Bono, look for the signposted access to the *Dolmen sa Coveccada* (131 E1) *(ɱ D7)*, the largest of its kind in the entire Mediterranean. The dolmen is in a field near a farmstead.

The church of the monastery of ★ ⚜ *San Pietro di Sorres* (131 D1–2) *(ɱ D7)* above Borutta was erected in the 12th century by Tuscan master builders and boasts the most ornately decorated façade of all the Sardinian Pisan churches, featuring inlays of colourful stones and filigree friezes. Inside, the light limestone walls contrast with the ceiling of black basalt.

The mighty structure rising in the centre of the broad valley floor is the nuraghi royal palace of *Santu Antine* (131 D2) (*M D7*) *(daily 9am–sunset)*. The central tower rises 14m/46ft above the triangular fort; embrasures and machicolations (to pour molten tar on attackers) are clearly visible. The dark corridors and stairs inside make you admire the ability of the master builders of the time who built with massive stones without much in the way of technical equipment – that are still standing after 2500 years. Explanations are provided by models and diagrams in the *Museo della Valle dei Nur-* *aghi* (April–Sept daily 9am–8pm, Oct–March 9am–5pm) in nearby Torralba. With its 20 rock tombs, the INSIDERTIP *Sant'Andria Priu necropolis* (131 E3) (*M D7*) *(daily 10am–1pm and 3pm–6pm, in summer to 7pm)* near Bonorva is one of the most impressive of its kind in Sardinia. Particularly spectacular is the *Tomba del Capo,* the chieftain's grave – at 2690ft2 the largest in Sardinia.

PORTO TORRES (124 B3) (*M C6*)

This sober port and industrial town just under 20km/12mi to the north-west doesn't really have much to offer apart from the basilica of *San Gavino,* a masterpiece of Romanesque church architecture that is also the island's largest sacred building. While the church was built in the 11th and 12th century, its columns were taken from Roman temples.

BOOKS & FILMS

▶ **My Father, My Master** – The true life story of Gavino Ledda from Siligo who was taken out of school as a child by his father to start a hard life as a shepherd boy, and only learned to read during military service, yet went on to teach at the university. The bestseller was turned into a film in 1977 with Nanni Moretti and shot by the brothers Paolo and Vittorio Taviani at the original locations. The Italian title is 'Padre Padrone'.

▶ **Bandits of Orgosolo** – This documentary-style, sensitively shot cinematic reportage (1961) in the tradition of Italian neo-realism by Vittorio de Seta is all about the people and their living conditions in the mountain villages of Sardinia.

▶ **Reeds in the Wind** – This novel is one of the few novels by the Nobel Prize winning author Grazia Deledda (and Sardinian native) to have been translated into English. Published in 1913 (Canne al vento) the novel tells movingly of Sardinia at the turn of the century.

▶ **The Advocate** – Advocate Bustianu likes to do things his own way, here he investigates the mysterious murder of a young woman. An exciting mystery – shortlisted for the Crime Writers Association Historical Dagger – by Marcello Fois whose protagonist works in and around early 20th century Nuoro, the birthplace of the author.

THE SOUTH

The fertile heart of the island is the extensive Campidano plain with endless wheat fields, vineyards and vegetable farms. In winter and spring the oranges ripen, early vegetables are grown under plastic coverings and hundreds of thousands of sheep graze on the stubble fields.

The Campidano plain, the ore-rich mountains around the old mining centre of Iglesias, the expansive basalt plateaus of the Barbagia Mountains and the undulating hills of the Marmilla have all been attracting conquerors since time immemorial when Sardinia was sought after for its silver and wheat. The large lagoon lakes of the Sinis Peninsula near Oristano, east of the island of Sant'Antioco and in the south-east around Muravera and the Flumendosa estuary, are abundant with birdlife and home

CITY **WHERE TO START?**
Following the signposts leading to 'Centro/Via Roma' takes you to the harbour, with the historic centre stretching out beyond. An ideal starting point is the large secure parking lot behind the railway station, where you can also hire a bike. From there it's only a short walk to the **Via Roma** boulevard. From here, you can explore into the maze of the Marina quarter, and head up to Castello, the old quarter of the nobility, at the centre of the three historic neighbourhoods of Marina, Stampace and Villanova.

Photo: Porto Pino beach

History was made here: the fertile plains and silver mines attracted conquerors and foreign rulers to the island

to cormorants, herons and flamingos. Santa Margherita di Pula, Villasimius and Muravera are popular holiday resorts; their charms lie in the small, scattered housing developments with a lot of greenery, the long sandy beaches and small coves and bays. Apart from a few heavily visited sections there is still a lot of space at the seaside, even in high season. The hills and the basalt plateaus act as veritable archaeological open air museums with nuraghi, well sanctuaries, menhirs and large stone circles, usually alone and remote in the vast landscape. Monte Linas, Sulcis and Sette Fratelli with their species-rich mountain forests are Unesco biosphere reserves. And Cagliari in the centre is a loud and vibrant – hectic even – Mediterranean port city.

CAGLIARI

MAP INSIDE BACK COVER
(127 D5) (*ω E12*) Sardinia's capital – and its seamlessly adjoining sur-

From the Bastione di San Remy on Cagliari's castle hill, the view goes far out to sea

rounding suburbs – has 370,000 inhabitants.

Old Cagliari occupies a commanding position on a rocky plateau above the Campidano plain, which at this point spreads
out to the sweeping Gulf of Cagliari, and
is bounded by lagoon lakes and salt flats.
When the Punics from North Africa land-
ed in Sardinia some 2700 years ago,
'Karalis' with its natural port was one of
the first settlements they founded.

Each historical period left its mark on
Cagliari's cityscape; the legacy of Punic
culture being subsumed into the subsequent Roman culture. Apart from the
medieval Castello with the cathedral, the
palaces of the archbishop, viceroy and
aristocratic families, today's old town is
dominated by baroque façades and
domes – three quarters of which are
around the castle mount. The city is built
on ten hills.

SIGHTSEEING

NATIONAL ARCHAEOLOGICAL MUSEUM (MUSEO ARCHEOLOGICO NAZIONALE) ★

The richest and most comprehensive collection of prehistoric and ancient finds in
Sardinia is housed in the new ● *Cittadel-
la dei Musei* (which includes an art museum with 16th/17th century Sardinian
paintings and three other museums) at
the highest point of the city. Most of the
space is taken up by the Nuragic culture;
the collection of small bronze statuettes
placed as votive offerings in the well
sanctuaries is impressive. Warriors, often
represented with four eyes, four arms,
two shields, are a frequent motif, others
are animals, mother goddesses and
boats with animals and people. *Tue–Sun
9am–7pm | Piazza Arsenale*

BOTANICAL GARDENS

Situated in the university quarter west of the city centre and below the amphitheatre, the *Orto Botanico* offers a good overview of Sardinian and Mediterranean flora. *April–Sept daily 8.30am–7pm Oct–March 8.30am–1.30pm | Via Fra Ignazio da Laconi*

CASTELLO

The old town on the hill is fortified like a castle and still has only two entrances, through either of the two city gates; between 10pm and 6am cars may only enter by special dispensation. The two tall towers, the *Torre San Pancrazio* and the *Torre dell'Elefante* with its stone elephants, were constructed by Pisan architects from the High Middle Ages. Today's access from Via Manno via the ☆ *Bastione di San Remy,* a meeting point for Cagliari's youngsters, was only created in the 19th century, when the viewing terraces were laid out.

The dark streets, lined by the tall palaces of the *Casteddu (*as the Sardinians call the castle quarter), is gradually taking on a new life, now attracting young artisans, goldsmiths and restorers to move into the houses and narrow courtyards that had were previously inhabited mainly by the old and poor. Only the broad Via Martini still conveys the image of its former glory, connecting the cathedral and the bishop's palace with the Piazza Indipendenza on the Torre San Pancrazio.

Climbing up to the castle is a steep and sweaty affair. But those who know the location of INSIDERTIP the three slightly hidden lifts up to the Castello may visit the quarter even in the heat of summer without getting out of breath. The lifts can be found above the Piazza Yenne next to the Santa Chiara church, as well as at the Viale Regina Elena, one near the Bastione San Remy, the other below the Piazza Palazzo.

CATTEDRALE (CATHEDRAL)

The columned façade (1933) was inspired by Pisa cathedral. The interior presents a heavy and extremely ornamental baroque. The numerous Spanish inscriptions are testimony to the fact that Sardinia once belonged to the Spanish Empire. The crypt, with its glorious baroque vault and 300 burial chambers, is particularly worth seeing. At the entrance to the cathedral is the marble Guglielmo pulpit featuring reliefs from the life of Jesus, which were created between 1159–62 for Pisa's cathedral. Once the Pisan pulpit by Giovanni Pisano was completed in 1311, the older piece was moved to Cagliari. *Mon–Fri 8am–noon and 2.30pm–8pm, Sat/Sun 8am–1pm and 4pm–8pm*

MARCO POLO HIGHLIGHTS

★ **National Archaeological Museum Cagliari**
Time travel into Nuragic culture, with fabulous views of the city and coast → p. 60

★ **Costa Verde**
Endless sandy beaches and dunes, most only accessible on foot → p. 68

★ **San Pietro**
The island is a Mediterranean paradise that offers a lot more than swimming and diving → p. 69

★ **Sinis Peninsula**
Steppe landscape with cliffs and deserted beaches; the lagoons provide a veritable Garden of Eden for herons, flamingos and seabirds → p. 71

SAN SATURNINO

The modest semi-domed edifice is Sardinia's oldest church, dating back to the 5th century, but It underwent alterations in the 11th and 12th centuries. Also known as Santi Cosma e Damiano, the church lies east of the city centre in a small park, surrounded by pine and palm trees.

SANTA MARIA DI BONARIA ☀

Those arriving by boat will get a full view of the church, with its mighty baroque façade and set of stairs, on a hill east of the city centre. This popular pilgrimage church also serves as a glorious viewpoint over the city and the wide Golfo degli Angeli. Legend has it that in 1370, an image of the Virgin Mary the stranded here, after being thrown overboard in a chest by a ship in distress. The Madonna became the patron saint of the fishermen and seafarers, and since 1908 has also been the official patron saint of the island of Sardinia. The numerous votive images in the cloister are a testimony to the great popularity and significance of this pilgrimage church.

FOOD & DRINK

Going out for a meal in Cagliari is always a special experience. All nuances of Sardinian cuisine are on offer: the traditional and the experimental, ingredients from the sea and the mountains. Those who want to just head off and go exploring should choose the Marina quarter with the Via Sardegna.

DAL CORSARO

This chic restaurant's dominant feature is its splendid art nouveau decor. The menu showcases innovative Sardinia cooking, using the whole cornucopia of fish, vegetables, and herbs. They also serve home-made wine. *Closed Sun | Viale Regina Margherita 28 | tel. 070 66 43 18 | Expensive*

FLORA

The elegant dining room is decorated with works of art. In addition to the seafood selection they also serve delicious farmhouse style vegetable dishes. *Closed Sun | Via Sassari 45 | tel. 070 66 47 35 | Moderate*

JANNAS

Very busy – just like in the old fishing days, and located right in the heart of the Marina quarter. *Closed Sun | Via Sardegna 85 | tel. 070 65 79 02 | Budget*

LISBOA

Small classy restaurant café with lounge bar that turns the freshest seasonal Sardinian produce into dishes that are as unusual as they are tasty. *Closed Fri | Via Tuveri 2 | tel. 07 04 37 07 | Moderate*

INSIDER TIP ▶ SEMPLICEMENTE

This hostaria is currently the undisputed star in Cagliari's gastronomic firmament. The young crew manages the culinary balancing act between tradition and modernity with enviable dexterity. Weekly rotating chefs with international credentials conjure up delicious dishes in a stylishly minimalist ambience. *Closed Fri | Viale Merello 60 | tel. 070 29 09 89 | www.ristorantesemplicemente.com | Moderate–Expensive*

SHOPPING

Luckily, the main shopping streets, Largo Carlo Felice and Via G. Manno, are still free of the international chains – instead there are numerous smaller fashion boutiques, shoe, lingerie, hat and tie shops. The *La Rinascente (Mon–Fri 9am–8.30pm,*

Sat 9am–9pm, Sun 10am–9pm) is Sardinia's high-end department store. This temple of consumption on Via Roma is steeped in tradition; it covers four floors long sandy beach, *Poetto* (with municipal bus connection) with typical Italian beach atmosphere: lidos with changing huts, bars and restaurants.

Cagliari's urban beach of Poetto has all the trimmings needed to enjoy Italian beach life

and carries numerous Italian design and fashion labels, shoe and perfume brands in addition to all the usual department store fare. Its best feature however is the ☕ *café* on the top floor, where you can enjoy fabulous views of the harbour while sipping a cappuccino. Delicacies from all over Sardinia can be purchased in sinfully expensive delis and in the slightly less expensive market halls. What is worthwhile are the **INSIDER TIP** gold and silversmiths in the Marina quarter *(Via Sardegna, Via Manno)* and the Castello quarter, offering some new very individual design alongside plenty of the more traditional ones.

BEACHES

Beyond the Capo Sant'Elia Peninsula in the south-east is the start of a 10km/6mi

WHERE TO STAY

Recent years have seen the emergence of numerous guest houses and bed & breakfasts in carefully restored historical buildings of the old town quarters, some of them very beautiful, and often with hotel-levels of comfort. There is a wide selection available and their facilities vary. For a good overview, consult *www.bbplanet.com/bed-and-breakfasts/cagliari/*

INSIDER TIP ▶ BED & BREAKFAST ANTICO PALAZZO CRISARIPAS

Exceedingly pretty rooms furnished in the Sardinian style in a historic 15th century palazzo in the Castello quarter, only a few steps away from the Piazza Indipendenza. Breakfast in the museum-like vault with well and cistern, served by the very charming and helpful hostess Sonja and her two daughters. *3 rooms | Via Canelles 104 | tel. 34 79 23 02 87 | www.crisaripa.it | Moderate*

ITALIA

Fine hotel in the Marina quarter. Book early! *113 rooms | Via Sardegna 31 | tel. 0 70 66 04 10 | www.hotelitaliacagliari.com | Moderate*

BED & BREAKFAST KASTRUM

Elegantly furnished B&B in a palace in the Castello quarter, with views over the old town. *6 rooms | Via Canelles 78 | tel. 0 70 66 23 04 | www.kastrum.eu | Moderate*

T-HOTEL ☆

This postmodern 65m/213ft glass tower is Cagliari's number one accommodation choice. Ultramodern futuristic design,

excellent cuisine, great breakfast, extremely professional staff and sublime views from the bright rooms. Ten minutes on foot to the city centre. *207 rooms | Via dei Giudicati 66 | tel. 07 04 74 00 | www.thotel.com | Expensive*

INFORMATION

Piazza Matteotti (railway station square) | tel. 0 70 66 92 55 | www.cagliariturismo.it

WHERE TO GO

CAMPIDANO
(126 B–C 2–4) (*ⅲ C–E 9–12*)

Large motorways lead right through the lagoons of the Stagno di Cagliari, so you see industrial chimneys instead of flamingos. The blindingly white salt hills of the salt pans provide raw material for the chemical industry. In the evening, young and old meet at the country church of Santa Maria on the outskirts of *Uta*. Continue on to *San Sperate,* where the first INSIDER TIP *murales* were painted in 1968. The village is like an open air museum, and its people are very proud of the more than 400 paintings.

COSTA DEL SUD AND THE HINTERLAND (126 C5–6) (*ⅲ D–E 13–14*)

The first 12km/7.5mi of this circular tour leads from Cagliari across the narrow isthmus dividing the open sea from the lagoon lakes and salinas or salt pans; then the Sulcis Mountains meet the coast, at first gently rolling, then a coastal plain and a long sandy beach.
This is where the Roman-Punic port town of *Nora* lies on a small peninsula; *most of its* columns, temple remains, mosaics and impressive theatre date from Roman Imperial era *(daily 9am–sunset).* Each summer, the theatre hosts the very popular ● *La Notte dei Poeti (www.lanottedei*

poeti.it) festival. Not far from the site and only a few steps from the spectacularly beautiful beach, the small friendly *su Gunventeddu hotel restaurant (9 rooms | tel. 07 09 20 90 92 | www.sugunventeddu. com | Budget–Moderate)* occupies the site of an old monastery and offers delicious seafood cuisine and a personal approach to hospitality.

Santa Margherita di Pula is a beach resort in a pine grove that extends over 5km/3mi. Exclusive villas and hotels alternate with holiday villages and campsites, beaches with plenty of space and well-equipped lidos. You can find almost everything here from bars to windsurf board hire: a golf course, clubs and a lot of traffic, but also the usual activities of a regular village. Right on the beach, the compact *is Morus* hotel *(55 rooms, 16 small villas | tel. 0 70 92 11 71 | www.ismorus.it | Expensive)* in set in lush gardens and has an interior decorated with Sardinian crafts.

Torre di Chia and the beach of the adjoining bay with its small lagoons appear like a vision: amongst dunes with juniper trees and rosemary shrubs and oleander, paths lead to the neighbouring bays, with a Saracen tower at the cape, and in its shadow the remains the Roman town of Bithia. Accommodation is available at the *su Giudeu* hotel *(20 rooms | tel. 07 09 23 02 60 | www.hotelsugiudeu.it | Budget–Moderate)* not far from the beach. The road runs along the coast, revealing small beach coves with tamarisks on the brook estuaries; trails and dirt roads lead to the ☆ *Capo Spartivento* foothills and the *Capo Malfatano,* Sardinia's southernmost point.

At the deep bay of Porto di Teulada, the road leaves the coast and carries on to *Teulada,* a large farming village amidst lush orange groves. 6km/3.5mi from the village is the *Agriturismo Matteu (10 rooms | tel. 07 09 27 00 03 | Budget)* set

2000 year old splendour: mosaic in Nora

amidst pastures and olive groves and serving tasty country cuisine from their own produce.

Carry on through rocky mountainous country towards Santadi. Halfway there you pass the *Grotta is Zuddas (April–Sept daily 9.30am–noon and 2.30pm–6pm, Oct–March Mon–Fri noon and 4pm, Sat/ Sun 9.30am–noon and 2.30pm–4pm | www.grotteiszuddas.com),* a stalactite cave worth seeing; at its entrance, an inviting locanda awaits, featuring a garden restaurant in a tranquil location.

Wine lovers should visit the *Cantina di Santadi winery (Via Cagliari 38 | tel. 078195 0127 | www.cantinadisantadi.it)* of which sells the sought-after INSIDER**TIP** Terre Brune cult wine, at relatively accessible prices.

MONTE ARCOSU (126 C5) (*Ø D12–13*)

Stretching west of the capital is the near-inaccessible and unpopulated Sulcis Mountain, an area of unspoilt nature that is a protected reserve. This is home to the *Monte Arcosu WWF reserve (www. ilcaprifoglio.it),* which is only open at weekends and offers a refuge to the *cervo sardo,* a small Sardinian deer threatened with extinction. At the entrance to the reserve are the starting points for several very beautiful hiking trails, of between two and eight hours duration.

IGLESIAS

(126 B4) (*Ø C12*) **Around the town, the traces of three thousand years of min-ing are conspicuous: Iglesias has been the capital of Sardinian metal process-ing for 800 years.**

Starting with silver, in the 19th century, followed by lead, zinc and copper, all were extracted and smelted. The discovery of large silver deposits in America spelled the temporary end for Sardinian mining. It took the resuming of extraction in the 19th century to have the population of Iglesias swell up to the 27,000 inhabitants it has today. The testimonies to mining activity – mining settlements, conveying machinery and slagheaps – were recognised in 2007 with a Unesco Geopark. They are currently being restored and made accessible to the public *(www.par cogeominerario.eu)*.

SIGHTSEEING

OLD TOWN

The old town of Iglesias, with partial remnants of its defensive city wall, offers an unexpected small-town experience: houses with pretty wrought iron balco-

View across the old town of Iglesias with the squat Romanesque cathedral in the foreground

nies, lots of colourful life in the streets, buildings that speak of the former wealth of a privileged town. The *cathedral* with its austere Romanesque façade dates back to the 13th century, as does the mendicant order church of *Santa Maria di Valverde,* a huge unadorned hall outside the walls. From the former town gate of Porta Sant'Antonio, one lane leads on to the ruined *Castello Salvaterra*, another to the mountain opposite with the pilgrimage church of *Nostra Signora del Buoncammino.*

MUSEO DELL'ARTE MINERARIA

Here you can take guided tours on mining and technology, and visit an exhibition mine. *Via Roma 47 | June Sat/Sun 6pm–8pm, July–Sept 6.30pm–8.30pm, at other times by appointment | tel. 07 81 35 00 37 | www.museoartemineraria.it*

FOOD & DRINK

VILLA DI CHIESA

Traditional Sardinian cooking right next to the medieval cathedral; tasty pasta and fish, with pizza served in the evenings as well. *Closed Mon except summertime | Piazza Municipio 9 | tel. 0 78 13 16 41 | Budget–Moderate*

WHERE TO STAY

EUROHOTEL

Restored palazzo on the edge on the old town, opulently furnished with the historical pomp from the town's golden times of the mining boom. *26 rooms | Via Fratelli Baniera 34 | tel. 0 78 13 40 78 | www.eurohoteliglesias.it | Moderate*

INFORMATION

Via Mazzini, corner of Via XXVII Marzo | tel. 07 81 27 44 48 | www.prolocoiglesias.it

WHERE TO GO

CARBONIA AND SULCIS

(126 B5–6) (*C12–13*)

Despite the closure of many mines, the triangle made up by Iglesias, Portoscuso, and Carbonia has remained an industrial area. Situated 25km/15.5 to the south, *Carbonia,* founded in 1938, it was built from the ground up during the Mussolini era. Mining of the lesser-quality brown coal has long been discontinued.

To the south-east, near the small town of Villaperuccio, is the exceptionally interesting yet little-known ● INSIDER TIP *Montessu necropolis (mid June–Aug daily 9am–1pm and 4pm–8pm, first half of June and first half of Sept 9am–1pm and 3pm–7pm, mid Sept–May 9am–5pm | www.montessu.it),* its diverse rock burial chambers extends over two hills, crisscrossed by numerous trails. Particularly spectacular are the two colossal royal tombs facing each other on the hills, their entrances designed to resemble faces.

In the port town of *Portoscuso* you can enjoy one of the best seafood experiences in all of Sardinia at the charming, elegant and exclusive INSIDER TIP *Ristorante La Ghinghetta (closed Sun and lunchtime | Via Cavour 26 | tel. 07 81 50 81 43 | www.laghinghetta.com | Expensive)* with eight guest rooms.

'Sensational' is no exaggeration when looking at the INSIDER TIP fantastic sandy beach belonging to the secluded hamlet of *Porto Pino*. The beach stretches for miles around the entire bay south of Punta Menga, adorned by a lagoon lake and with its fine, blindingly white sand and dunes it resembles a desert. And indeed, it is desert wars that Nato are training for in a huge military restricted zone, comprising the whole of Capo Teulada. In summer however, the prettiest part of the beach, on the southern side of the bay, is opened to visitors.

For many years this was the top insiders' tip for Sardinian travellers tired of city life, who would pack the car full of tinned food, roll out their sleeping bags on the beach and stay for weeks. Most of the endless sandy and dune beaches south of Marina di Arbus (75km/46mi north of Iglesias) are only accessible on foot. In *Torre dei Corsari* at Porto Palma, above enormous red-yellow dunes, the *La Caletta* hotel *(32 rooms | tel. 0 70 97 70 33 | www.lacaletta.it | Moderate)* is situated within one of the new holiday villages. South of the (not very appealing) Marina di Arbus holiday village – beyond which the road turns into a rough track that is not always passable – marks the start of the nature reserve with a beach that runs on for miles, with sand dunes up to 300m/ 985ft high. The track in the Riu Piscinas valley leads to derelict mining villages. At the Piscinas estuary, the unique INSIDERTIP *Le Dune* hotel restaurant *(25 rooms | tel. 0 70 97 71 30 | www.leduneingurtosu.it | Expensive)* is right on the beach in restored warehouses that used to serve the 19th century mines.

INSIDERTIP **FLUMINESE**
(126 B4) (*⊘ C11–12*)

The white lime cliffs and mountain chains, the old holm oak forests with many wild boars, the huge slag heaps, ghost villages and – once off the state road to Fluminimaggiore – jeep tracks, lie in a region that is unknown even to most Sardinians.

A side road leads to the *Temple of Antas,* a sanctuary from the mixed Roman-Punic culture. A narrow back road leads from *Portixeddu* with its long sandy beach out to the wild 🌿 *Capo Pecora,* where you can have wonderful views back to the coast.

Against a backdrop of vertical mountain flanks, derelict mines and slag heaps, the former mine worker village of *Buggerru* is attempting to lure in tourists with its new marina and the former mine *Galleria Henry (guided tours Mon–Fri 9am–1pm and 2.30pm–4pm, Sat/Sun 9am–1pm),* which was reopened as an exhibition mine. For accommodation and fabulous views over the bay of Portixeddu, head for the organic farm 🌿 ⏰ *Agriturismo La Fighezia (6 rooms | Fighezia part of town | tel. 34 80 69 83 03 | www.agriturismofighezia.it, Budget–Moderate)* in an eco-friendly building.

As pretty as a picture is the beach cove of *Cala Domestica,* which you pass on the drive south, which still has some derelict ore loading facilities. Negotiating some extreme ascents and descents, the road leads to *Masua,* which is also dominated by derelict mines and mining relics. Masua overlooks the picturesque *Pan di Zucchero,* a mighty rock islet just off the coast. In the neighbouring village of *Nebida,* nestled on the steep mountain slope high above the sea, is the *Albergo Trattoria Pan di Zucchero (14 rooms | Via Centrale 365 | tel. 0 78 14 71 14 | Budget)* which offers excellent cuisine at fair prices, one of the reasons it is a popular meeting place for the locals. The best thing about Nebida though is the ● rock bar *Al 906 Operaio (closed Mon)* – on the 🌿 Belvedere, one of the most beautiful places on the island to sit back and experience the sunset in all its glory.

At Domusnovas is the ● *Grotta di San Giovanni* stalactite cave which up until recently had a road running through it. It is now closed to traffic and visitors may explore it on foot in 20 minutes, following the babbling mountain brook which once formed it. The end of the cave marks the beginning of the wild mountain terrain of the *Parco Regionale Monte Linas-Oridda-Marganai* – it is uninhabited but features numerous historic mines and remnants of the mining boom.

SANT'ANTIOCO AND SAN PIETRO
(126 A–B 5–6) (*∭ B–C13*)

Sant'Antioco is separated from the mainland by a shallow estuary and lagoons; the dam and bridge date back to the

0781810188 | www.hotelstelladelsud.com | *Moderate*) has gardens, a pool and tennis court.

Every two hours or so, a ferry runs to the neighbouring island of ★ *San Pietro*. This volcanic island is a world all unto its own. Its inhabitants are Ligurians who emigrated centuries ago from their

Tuna fishing on San Pietro: a controversial tradition

ancient Romans. The town of *Sant'Antioco* (40km/25mi south of Iglesias) is a busy Mediterranean port at the site of the Punic-Roman Sulcis, where silver and lead – from the mines on the mainland opposite – was shipped. Above the town, at the 18th century fort, a villa houses a *museum (daily 9am–7pm)*, displaying the finds from the necropolis and the tophet – a ritual site where children were sacrificed to deities.

In the same way as the island of San Pietro opposite, *Calasetta* is inhabited by Ligurian immigrants. The friendly village boasts a fine bathing beach, the *Spiaggia Grande*. Right on the beach, the *Stella del Sud* hotel (49 rooms | tel.

homeland near Genova to North Africa, keeping their language and traditions, to then went settle on San Pietro in the 18th century.

The main settlement of *Carloforte* is a picturesque fishing village with a lot of charm and flair. A few of the bays between the imposing cliffs of volcanic basalt are suitable for bathing. However, visitors don't come to Carloforte for the swimming, but for its special cuisine. This is where *tonno* (tuna) has been caught since time immemorial and where it is on the menu at numerous restaurants. Two recommended restaurants are *Al Tonno di Corsa (closed Mon | Via Marconi 47 | tel. 0781855106 | www.tonnodicorsa.it |*

Moderate) in the heart of the old town, and *Da Nicolo (May–Oct daily | Corso Cavour 32 | tel. 07 81 85 40 48 | www.danicolo.net | Moderate–Expensive)*, serving tuna specialities in an ancient vault in the winter, and outdoors on the seafront promenade in summer. Owner and head chef Luigi Pomata (a well known Italian television celebrity) managing this third generation establishment, has won several awards. For accommodation, look no further than the charming *Hotel Hieracon (23 rooms | Corso Cavour 62 | tel. 07 81 85 40 28 | www.hotelhieracon.com | Moderate)* housed in an old palazzo. For more information: *Corso Tagliafico 2 | tel. 07 81 85 40 09 | www.prolococarloforte.it*

ORISTANO

(126 B2) (*⍰ C9*) The provincial capital (pop. 32,000) lies at the mouth of the Tirso River at the start of the Campidano plain.
The historic centre within the town walls has a peaceful ambience. Having experienced its heyday as the capital of the Arborea giudicato in the 14th century, it declined under Spanish rule to a provincial diocese.

OLD TOWN
The *Porta Mannu* with the late medieval San Cristoforo tower marks the main entrance to the old town. In the mornings, a lively *farmers' market* is held on the Piazza Roma. The Piazza Eleonora d'Arborea with the monument of the national heroine is on the way to the wide Piazza Duomo with its neoclassical *San Francesco* church.

FOOD & DRINK

IL FARO
Classic art nouveau furnishings and top regional cuisine. *Closed Sun | Via Bellini 25 | tel. 0 78 37 00 02 | Moderate–Expensive*

TRATTORIA GINO
Right in the heart of things, lively and always popular, thanks to its simple yet tasty food. *Closed Sun | Via Tirso 13 | tel. 0 78 37 14 28 | Budget–Moderate*

WHERE TO STAY

INSIDER TIP HOTEL DUOMO
Small charming four star hotel in a 16th century palazzo with antique interior and dignified flair. *10 rooms | Via Vittorio Emanuele II 34 | tel. 07 83 77 80 61 | www.hotelduomo.net | Moderate*

INSIDER TIP HOSTEL RODIA
Modern guest house 500m outside the old town, with bright generous rooms and the comforts you'd expect of a hotel. Internet access. *69 rooms | Prolungamento Viale Repubblica 103 | tel. 07 83 25 18 81 | www.hostelrodia.it | Budget*

INFORMATION

Piazza Eleonora d'Arborea 19 | tel. 0 78 33 68 32 10 | www.oristanoturismo.it

WHERE TO GO

CAMPIDANO AND MARMILLA
A few steps lead to the church in the southern suburb of *Santa Giusta* **(126 B2) (*⍰ C10*)**. The church's classically simple façade hides a light-filled Romanesque interior; the three naves are supported by Roman columns from Tharros. Lagoon lakes and narrow promontories are a reminder of the malaria-ridden

coastal swamps which were drained by settlers from northern Italy after 1920.

In the hills below the Giara di Gesturi plateau, side roads lead through tiny villages, where time seems to have stood still, to *Villanovaforru* (126 C3) *(ɲ D11).* 1km from the village is the *Genna Maria* nuragic castle; important finds are exhibited in the village *museum (Tue–Sun*

mullet *(muggine)* formed the basis for the fishermen's survival, which was always hard, even though the mullet is sought after for its roe from which the Sardinian 'caviar', *bottarga* is made.

The unremarkable small fishing town (pop. 9000) is the best place on the island to eat fish. Several restaurants offer seafood in such high quality and degree

National heroine Eleonora d'Arborea guarding the Oristano square named after her

9.30am–1pm and 3.30pm–7pm), providing glimpses of Sardinian history with reconstructions, timelines, overview maps and a folk art exhibition. If you want to stay over then the appealing *Le Colline* hotel *(20 rooms | tel. 0709300123 | Moderate)* at the nuraghe is a good option.

SINIS PENINSULA ★
(126 B1–2) *(ɲ C9–10)*

Cabras enjoys a position on an inland body of water well known for its rich fishing grounds. The *Stagno di Cabras* is connected with the sea by channels. Brackish water fish such as eel *(anguilla)* and

of freshness that people come all the way from Cagliari to eat here. For some excellent food try *Sa Zibba (closed Tue | Via Leopardi 53 | tel. 0783392023 | www. ristorantesazibba.com | Moderate)* or *Zia Beledda (closed Tue | Via Amsicora 43 | tel. 0783290801 | Moderate).* Still largely undiscovered by tourists, the sandy flat beach of *Torre Grande* with its fine sand and lido, while *Da Giovanni (closed Mon | tel. 0783220 51 | Moderate)* serves delicious seafood.

Further west, the barren uninhabited *Sinis* Peninsula stretches out. In summer, the saline lakes in the immeasurably vast plain often dry out; from autumn onwards, thousands of flamingos spend winter in the ankle-deep water. Parts of the coast and the dunes, covered with dwarf palm trees, are a bird sanctuary and may only be entered accompanied by nature guides working for the WWF and the Lipu bird conservation association (more information on site). At San Giovanni, is Arutas and Mari Ermi the coast is flat and quartz pebble beaches alternate with razor-sharp stone cliffs. In some parts the sandstone plate drops off in 10–20m/33–66ft cliffs.

San Salvatore forms a low group of houses amidst the steppe. In September, the tiny church with the pre-Christian crypt becomes the destination of the Corsa degli Scalzi barefoot pilgrimage run. Before you get to the cape, at the end of the road, are some low holiday chalets and fishing huts – here still built from reeds – clustered around the pre-Christian church of *San Giovanni*. Accommodation and food are available the *Sinis Vacanze Sa Pedrera (14 rooms | tel. 07 83 37 00 40 | www.sapedrera.it | Moderate)*, a bungalow hotel managed by young dedicated environmentalists. On

the narrow isthmus, *Tharros (daily 9am–8pm, in winter 9am–5pm | www.tharros. info)* is the island's largest Punic-Roman town with well preserved streets (with the drainage running in the centre between the basalt paving), residential quarters, temples and thermal baths.

In the north of the Sinis Peninsula, near the villages of Putzu Idu and su Pallosu, where the better beaches are only accessible on foot, is the *Da Cesare* hotel *(9 rooms | tel. 0 78 35 20 95 | Moderate)* that also serves fine seafood. In the north, up to the steep coast at Santa Caterina di Pittinuri, beach pine forests cover dunes on *is Arenas* beach. In the village, the hotel restaurant *La Scogliera (7 rooms | tel. 0 78 53 82 31 | www.hotel-lascogliera.it | Budget–Moderate)* is situated on the bay.

TIRSO VALLEY AND THE ABBASANTA PLATEAU

North of Oristano marks the start of the Abbasanta plateau which is rich in archaeology. From the motorway, just under 30km/18.5mi north, an exit leads to *Santa Cristina* (131 D6) *(ɱ D9)* an extensive archaeological site with bar and

Poignant simplicity: San Giovanni di Sinis has its roots in the 6th/7th centuries

restaurant set amidst an olive grove next to a Nuragic village. The village has round huts and nuraghe, as well as an early Christian church and the very well preserved subterranean INSIDER TIP *Santa Cristina well sanctuary (daily 8.30am–sunset)* dating as far back as the 12th century BC, which counts amongst Sardinia's most splendid prehistoric monuments. With its 13m/42ft tower visible from afar, the nearby *Nuraghe Losa (daily 9am–sunset)* is one of the best preserved in Sardinia.

Cork oaks, wild olives, nuraghi and endless walls accompany the drive to ☆ *Santu Lussurgiu (130 C5–6) (⌂ D8)* 15km/9mi west of Abbasanta. The main attraction of the mountain village is the *Cascata Sos Molinos,* a picturesque waterfall, where the mill stream (about 1km out of the village below the road to Bonarcado) plunges dramatically into a small, lush gorge. The ☺ *La Bocca del Vulcano (daily | Via Alagon 27 | tel. 0783 55 09 74 | www.laboccadelvulcano.it | Budget)* is entirely committed to regional cuisine and the Slow Food philosophy, also organising hikes and horse-

back excursions. A dream accommodation choice is the ☺ *Antica Dimora del Gruccione (8 rooms | Via Obinu 31 | tel. 0783 55 20 35 | www.anticadimora.com | Moderate),* housed in an old palazzo in the heart of the historic centre. It is not only the building with its lovely courtyard and the food that deserve praise, but also Gabriella Belloni, a dedicated follower of the Slow Food movement, and her two charming daughters who take excellent care of their guests.

Another 18km/11mi north-west, the high up neighbouring village of ☆ INSIDER TIP *Cuglieri (130 C5) (⌂ C8)* offers superb views of the coast towards the north, the highlands of Abbasanta and Macomer and beyond to the mountains of the Barbagia. In the historic centre of the old town, the *Meridiana (closed Wed | Via Littorio 1 | tel. 0 78 53 94 00 | Moderate)* serves fine antipasti and a wide selection of fish and seafood.

Thanks to its numerous ice-cold springs in a dense holm oak grove, *San Leonardo de Siete Fuentes (131 D5) (⌂ D8)* is a favourite place for Sardinians to escape to for some respite from the summer heat. Via *Borore,* surrounded by a wealth of nuraghi, giant tombs and stone circles, the road carries on to *Sedilo (131 E–F5) (⌂ D8),* a shepherd's village above the Tirso reservoir lake, well known for the pilgrimage church of *Sant'Antine* dedicated to Saint Constantine, the patron saint of accidents. Situated 2km/1.2mi outside the village, high above the lake, the interior walls of the church are covered with INSIDER TIP countless votive offerings, some quite strange – accidents averted at the last minute and other mishaps – which make a wander round the church quite amusing and interesting.

Entirely built from red natural stone *Fordongianus (126 C1) (⌂ D9)* was already an important site for the Romans, who called it Forum Traiani. On the river, you'll see the walls of the ● *Roman thermal baths (May–Sept Tue–Sun 9am–1pm and 3pm–7.30pm, Oct–April 9.30am–1pm and 2.30pm–5.30pm)*, with 60 °C/140 °F hot springs.

VILLASIMIUS

(127 E5) (Ⓜ F13) **Over the years, the former shepherd's village (pop. 2600) has turned into a popular holiday destination which includes the wonderful beaches around Capo Carbonara, Cala Sinzias, Costa Rei and Capo Ferrato, as well as the granite mountains of the Sette Fratelli.** Back roads lead to the beaches and into the holiday resorts where gardens form oases in the bare granite landscape.

FOOD & DRINK

DA BARBARA
11km/7mi west of Villasimius, near Solanas at km 27/16mi on the road to Cagliari, this eatery has for generations been attracting guests with its fresh fish and easy-going atmosphere. *Closed Wed out of season | tel. 0 70 75 06 30 | Moderate*

CARBONARA
Unless you decide to order the crayfish, enjoy good seafood at reasonable prices. *Closed Wed | Via Umberto I 60 | tel. 0 70 79 12 70 | Moderate*

BEACHES

No other place can boast so many and such varied beaches. *Porto Giunco* (access via the Capo Carbonara road) provides a picture-postcard idyll between the sea and a lagoon lake. The gorgeous beach of *Punta Molentis* (near the SP 18 in the direction of Costa Rei) connects the mainland with an off-shore rocky is-

let. *Campus* is the name of the pretty sandy bay near the Hotel Cormoran on the SP 17 in the direction of Cagliari. From the Campus beach, a short footpath leads to the splendid *Cuccureddus* beach. Softly curved and framed by picturesque rock cliffs is the long *Cala Pira* on the SP 18 towards Costa Rei. *Cala Monte Turno* lies in beautiful nature between picturesque rock cliffs near Cala Sinzias; a fabulous snorkelling spot!

WHERE TO STAY

CRUCCURIS RESORT
Fairly new complex in the hills behind the town, with three swimming pools. *49 rooms | tel. 07 07 98 90 20 | www.cruccurisresort.com | Moderate–Expensive*

INSIDER TIP L'OLEANDRO
Secluded location in a valley that leads to the sea, managed with commitment and a personal touch. *9 rooms | 3km/1.8mi on the road leading to Costa Rei | tel. 0 70 79 15 39 | Budget–Moderate*

STELLA D'ORO
Run by the same family since 1929, this village hotel has hardly changed. *17 rooms | tel. 0 70 79 12 55 | www.hotel.stelladoro@virgilio.it | Moderate*

INFORMATION

Piazza Giovanni XXIII | tel. 07 07 93 02 71 | www.villasimiusweb.com

WHERE TO GO

COSTA REI ● *(127 E4–5) (Ⓜ F–G12)*
Towards the north, the coast remains rough and rocky up to Cala Sinzias, and then it changes to long sandy beaches. More than 10km/6mi long, the Costa Rei is only developed in parts but unfortu-

nately those are huge holiday resorts and bungalow complexes. A detour well worth doing leads to the sandy bay of Porto Pirastu and Capo Ferrato, where the wide sandy beach turns into coastal cliffs. Further north, from San Priamo onwards, the coastal road runs past large lagoon lakes with herons, cormorants and flamingos.

MURAVERA, VILLAPUTZU AND SARRABUS (127 E4) (*F–G11*)

Surrounded by lush orange groves, the two large villages on the estuary of the Flumendosa appear quite forbidding at first with their flat windowless houses. In the past, life would be played out in the courtyards – exactly the kind of romantic courtyard you can experience and enjoy in the ☺ *B & B Su Pasiu (6 rooms | Via Speranza 8 | tel. 34 06 19 81 88 | www.bed-and-breakfast-costarei.com | Moderate)*, housed in a very tastefully restored historic manor house in the centre of the village. The house was restored with natural materials from the region and furnished with traditional objects. Wonderfully fresh fish and mussels can be had in neighbouring Villaputzu in the trattoria *Su Talleri*

(closed Sun evening | tel. 0 70 99 75 74 | Moderate) at the turn off to Porto Corallo. 23km/14mi further inland, in Villasalto, a place to enjoy traditional Sardinian cuisine with cheese, ricotta, game, lamb and kid goat is the INSIDER TIP *Osteria di Paolo Perella (closed Mon | Corso Repubblica 8 a | tel. 0 70 95 62 98 | Moderate)*. In his kitchen, Paolo prepares rare, almost forgotten traditional recipes from foraged ingredients such as mushrooms, wild fennel or wild asparagus.

One of the most beautiful areas for family hikes and mountain biking in Sardinia is the ● *Parco Sette Fratelli (entrance SS 125 km 30.1)* in the Sarrabus, which is crisscrossed by attractively landscaped trails. There are idyllic picnic spots, and an educational trail through the *Botanical Gardens of Maidopis (May–Sept daily 7am–6pm, Oct–April 7am–3pm)* that presents the flora of the region. At the entrance to the freely accessible park there are free maps marking the trails, as well as the *Museo Cervo Sardo (March–Oct Tue–Sun 10am–noon and 2pm–5pm, Nov–Feb Sat/Sun 10am–1pm)*, with information about the exceedingly rare Sardinian deer, a few of which are still living in the park.

Endless sandy beaches at the Costa Rei on Sardinia's south-eastern tip

THE EAST COAST

The *Orientale Sarda*, the 125 national road from Cagliari to Palau via Tortolì, Dorgali and Olbia, is the Sardinian dream drive; you'll be hard pressed to find a straight line for more than a few miles of its 355km/220mi.

While the road nearly always runs within few miles' distance from the sea, high impassable mountains block the view and access. Apart from narrow coastal plains and river estuaries, the mountains reach all the way down to the coast.

In the Gulf of Orosei, the limestone massif of the Supramonte marks a vertical drop of up to 600m/1960ft down to the sea. The only access by land is on foot – a day's walk over hill and dale – through deep gorges to remote coves, which are however, frequented by numerous excursion boats during the short season. This part of the coast forms a national park, together with the mountains of the Barbagia that reach deep into the interior. North of Orosei, pine-studded white sandy bays alternate with cliffs. Despite encroaching tourist development, there are still long deserted sections. The seaside resorts of the east coast serve as a good base for day trips into the interior.

ARBATAX AND TORTOLÌ

(127 F2) *(ſ G9)* **Arbatax (pop. 1100) is situated on a peninsula, its striking red porphyry cliffs form one of the natural wonders of Sardinia.**

Photo: Grotta del Bue Marinoni near Cala Gonone

Between the sea and the mountains:
long bays with pale sand, coastal towers,
cliffs, gorges and sea grottoes

Most of this rocky tip is not accessible as several holiday colonies and the military occupy nearly the whole area, so that the ascent to the ☀ lighthouse ends at a barrier fence.

Tortolì (pop. 9000) 5km/3mi inland is the 'capital' of Ogliastra, the countryside between Sardinia's high mountains, falling in a dramatic vertical drop down to the plain and the hill country around Bari Sardo; until the point where the mountains reach down all the way to the sea between Marina di Gairo and Quirra. Long sandy beaches with pine trees and tamarisks lie to the south. The clean sandy beach of *Porto Frailis* in Arbatax is often overrun.

Seafood delicacies and generous portions ensure a steady revolving door at *Del Porto (closed Mon | Arbatax | Via Bellavista 14 | tel. 07 82 66 72 26 | Budget)*. For simple and welcoming accommodation try the *Albergo Da Angelo (6 rooms | Tortolì | Via Piemonte 15 | tel. 07 82 62 35 33 | Budget)*. A prime example of romantically ornate neo-Sardinian architecture is the charming *La Bitta (41 rooms | Ar-*

Sardinian natural wonder: the red porphyry cliffs of Arbatax

batax | tel. *07 82 66 70 80* | *www.hotella bitta.it* | *Expensive*) right on the beach of Porto Frailis, where no room resembles the other. The hotel's fine cuisine matches its style and sophistication.

For more information: *Tortolì | Via Cedrino 24 | tel. 07 82 66 00 00 | www.turismo. ogliastra.it*

WHERE TO GO

BARI SARDO AND MARINA DI GAIRO (127 F2) (*Ø G10*)

On the drive south, Bari Sardo is the first place to offer the opportunity to reach the sea. *Marina di Bari* has a long, wide sandy beach. A few hotels and campsites cluster around the coastal towers. The leading hotel here is the elegant *La Torre* (60 rooms | tel. *0 78 22 80 30* | *www.ho tellatorresardegna.it* | *Moderate–Expensive*), built in a Sardinian-Moorish style.

A gravel road runs through the coastal plain, but at a distance from the sea, to the little country church of *Nostra Signora del Buon Cammino* where it turns into as-

phalt and leads from the state road to the ★ *Marina di Gairo.* While the sandy beach is flat to start with, the coast becomes increasingly more dramatic; small coves with colourful pebbles and sandy sections lie between the long, bright red cliff promontories, porphyry islets and rock needles: this is a beach in its natural state.

BAUNEI, SANTA MARIA NAVARRESE AND SU GOLGO (127 F1) (*Ø G9*)

In the north of the Ogliastra plain, the Supramonte Mountains push down, dropping towards the sea and the plain as a mass of rock over 1000m/3280ft in height. *Lotzorai* and *Donigala* have flat, sandy beaches, ending abruptly at the dramatic coast of ● *Santa Maria Navarrese.* In front of the church, stop to admire several olive trees that are over 1000 years old. Right above the beach, the *L'Olivastro* bar awaits below the huge crown of one of the ancient olive trees. The farming and fishing village wending its way up the mountain boasts an enticing amount of greenery and flowers. Accommodation can be had in private rooms, holiday apartments and friendly, quiet hotels, such as the *Santa Maria (37 rooms | tel. 0782 615315 | www.albergosantamaria.it | Moderate)* or the *Aggiustra (19 rooms | tel. 0782 6150 05 | www.hotelagugliastra.it | Moderate)*. Excursion boat trips run along the dramatic coast to secluded coves. For more information: *Piazza Principessa di Navarra 19 | Santa Maria Navarrese | tel. 0782 615330 | www.turinforma.it*

The road then winds its way up high through a rocky landscape. The detour to the rocky cape of ⚜ **INSIDER TIP** *sa Pedra Longa* is well worth doing. Stepped paths lead down to the water but swimming from the cliffs is only possible when the sea is calm.

The mountain village of *Baunei* stretches along the road on a narrow terrace high above the plain, dominated by rock cliffs. It's a 12km/9mi drive on a winding asphalt road again to reach the high *su Golgo* plateau, where in early July the small remote country church of San Pietro turns into a fairground with a wild horserace and banquet under the tall trees. A ten minute walk on a path takes you to *su Sterru* a 270m/885ft deep natural sinkhole in the limestone karst. Rural fare can be had at the *Locanda Il Rifugio – Golgo* hostel *(25 beds in 6 1–4 bed dorms | daily | tel. 3687 02 89 80 | www.coopgoloritze. com | Budget)*, which marks the start of marked trails and also the point where horse-riding tours, guided hikes, gorge and climbing tours are organised, into the *Codula di Sisine* –ending as a deep gorge on the splendid *Cala Sisine* – as well as into the beautiful bay of *Cala Goloritzè*.

LANUSEI AND THE OGLIASTRA MOUNTAINS (127 E2) (*ω F9–10*)

Halfway up, rising from the plain and the barren hills with their sparse maquis, the road reaches fertile garden country. Here

there are babbling brooks and small villages hidden in the lush greenery of fruit trees. ⚜ *Villagrande Strisaili* is the belvedere of Ogliastra. Passing a dense holm oak forest with ice-cold springs, the road reaches *Lake Flumendosa,* with the Gennargentu massif rising majestically beyond. Then it goes downhill to *Arzana.* At the centre of this large friendly village, the comfortable Hotel *Murru (30 rooms | tel. 078 23 76 65 | www.hotelmurru.com | Budget)* serves typically Sardinian fare. *Lanusei* is the old capital of the Ogliastra, and its steep streets and tall houses lend it a very urban appearance. The central, simple ⚜ hotel *Belvedere (10 rooms | tel. 078 24 21 84 | www.belvederelanusei.it | Budget–Moderate)* truly lives up to its name.

DORGALI AND CALA GONONE

The shepherd and farming town of Dorgali is tucked away in the mountains

From *Ulassai*, picturesquely situated below jagged rocks, a narrow road leads through the rock up to the spectacular stalactite cave, *Grotta su Marmuri (guided tours April and Oct daily 11am, 2.30pm, 5pm, May–July and Sept 11am, 2pm, 4pm, 6pm, Aug 11am, 1pm, 3pm, 5pm, 6.30pm)*.

BEACHES (127 F1–2) (*GO G9–10*)

The *Spiaggia Cea* forms a wonderful sandy bay, with off-shore rock needles of red porphyry, on the side street to Torre di Bari. The intensely picturesque beach at *Lido di Orrì* is miles long and dotted by rocks polished into round shapes. **INSIDER TIP** *Cala Goloritzè* and *Cala Mariolu* are two of the most beautiful sandy bays in Sardinia. Situated on the steep coast, they can only be accessed by boat. However, Cala Goloritzè can also be reached from the su Golgo high plateau by descending a hiking trail starting at Baunei. The picture-perfect beach of *Lotzorai* with its belt of dunes and shady pine trees stretches for miles.

TRENINO VERDE ★ �^
(127 D–F2) (*GO F–G 9–10*)

Meaning 'little green train' the small narrow gauge bears its name for a good reason, it snakes its way via countless hairpin bends through the wild, lush, green mountain country of the Ogliastra and Barbagia. While the little train ran to a regular schedule up to a few years ago, today it only services the most scenic part from Arbatax to Mandas, with a detour to Sorgono between June and September twice a day (except Tue) for tourists. The Isili–Sorgono stretch is only served once a day on a Tuesday.

A lovely day trip runs Saturdays and Sundays (more frequently in high summer) from Arbatax *(departing at 8am)* to Sadali *(arriving 11.28am)*, where you can visit the Grotta de is Janas cave (see 'The Interior') and then catch the 5.10pm train back to Arbatax *(arriving 8.30pm)*. For more information: *tel. 0 70 58 02 46 | www.treninoverde.com*

DORGALI AND CALA GONONE

(125 E–F5) (*GO G8*) **Hidden behind mountains, the large shepherd and farming town of Dorgali (pop. 8000) was not visible from the sea and thus protected from pirates and the Saracens.** The Dorgalese show their colourful costumes and the filigree jewellery – famous all over Sardinia – at their three large religious festivities at Easter, mid August at San Giuseppe and on 15th September. The �^ magnificent panoramic road, offering vistas of the mountains and coast of the Supramonte, starts off through a tunnel and then goes in endless serpen-

tines to Cala Gonone. Cala Gonone is a holiday resort that consists almost exclusively of hotels and holiday villas, but it has no big buildings, lots of greenery and a narrow man-made beach.

FOOD & DRINK – WHERE TO STAY

COSTA DORADA

On the Cala Gonone beach, nicely furnished, and featuring terraces with flowers and views of the steep coast. *28 rooms | tel. 0 78 49 33 32 | www.hotelcostadorada.it | Moderate–Expensive*

AGRITURISMO DIDONE

In a quiet and secluded location between Orosei and Dorgali, this organic *agriturismo* farm offers a splendid panoramic view of the coast. Why not try the 'Antidieta' menu, catering for everybody who shares the owners' conviction that living healthily also means having fun eating. Only a short drive away from the dream beaches of Cala Osalla and Cala Cartoe. *14 rooms | sa Carruba part of town | tel.* *34 03 79 19 36 | www.agriturismodidone.com | Moderate*

OASI

High above the town and the sea, with fabulous views. *30 rooms | Cala Gonone | tel. 0 78 49 31 11 | www.loasihotel.it | Budget–Expensive*

SANT'ELENE

Simple country hotel in a quiet, secluded location and serving fine regional cooking. *8 rooms | tel. 0 78 49 45 72 | www.hotelsantelene.it | Budget*

SPORTS & BEACHES

Marked hiking trails connect Dorgali with Cala Gonone, and lead deep into the Supramonte to the beach coves of *Cala Cartoe* and *Cala Osalla* in the north and *Cala Fuili* and *Cala Luna* (also served by boats) in the south. Those with no mountaineering experience and equipment can reach the gorge of *su Gorruppu* and *Tiscali*, but no further.

Many of the bathing bays and coves near Cala Gonone can only be accessed by boat

Dorgali: Via Lamarmora | tel. 0 78 49 62 43; Cala Gonone: Viale Bue Marino | tel. 0 78 49 36 96; www.dorgali.it

WHERE TO GO

INSIDER TIP CODULA DI LUNA
(125 E6) (*ØJ F–G8*)

The most spectacular and most remote stretch of the 125 road lies between Dorgali and Baunei. 46km/28mi divide the two towns, the road reaching its highest point at the ☼ *Genna Silana*, 1017m/3336ft above sea level. On the vast high plateau above Urzulei, with water courses where herds of horses roam free and graze from spring to late autumn, 2.5km/1.5mi beyond the turn to Urzulei, a narrow tarred road turns off to the left, leading into the Codula valley and ending

in Teletotes. There, the valley becomes so narrow that you can only proceed on foot on trails and the scree bed of the gorges (note that it will take six to eight hours to the sea and back; you'll definitely need a good level of physical fitness, hiking gear and drinking water to do this).

SU GORRUPPU AND TISCALI
(125 E6) (*ØJ F8*)

Arising at the Arcu Correboi at the foot of the Gennargentu, the Flumineddu breaks through Monte Oddeu (over 1000m/3280ft) in the gorge of ★ *su Gorruppu*. The vertical walls of the gorge are 200m/656ft high, only a few yards wide at its most narrow points. From Dorgali, a tarmac road leads to the bridge of Ponte Barva, from where a footpath (about two hours) leads to the entrance of the gorge. Also from Ponte Barva, a walk – on a marked footpath *at times* rocky and difficult – takes two hours to reach the Stone Age cave village of *Tiscali (daily 9am–1pm and 3pm–7pm)*. Once hidden in a gigantic rock chamber, and impossible for strangers to find, the collapsed roof now sheds some light on to one of the Nuragic people's last refuges.

GROTTA DEL BUE MARINO
(125 E–F6) (*ØJ G8*)

Of the 5km/3mi of the grotto that has already been explored, 900m/300ft is open to the public: watch for the sublime interplay of colours between the water and the stalactites and stalagmites. Access is by boat from Cala Gonone.

GROTTA DI ISPINIGOLI ★ ●
(125 E–F5) (*ØJ G8*)

The descent in the cave shaft leads past a stalagmite (38m/125ft tall) into a fantasy world of stalactite-stalagmite galleries and halls, lit up in many colours. *Hourly guided tours, April–Sept daily*

THE EAST COAST

9am–7pm, Oct–March Mon–Fri 11am and noon, Sat/Sun 11am, noon and 3pm

OROSEI (125 F5) (*Ø G7*)

This small town, (pop. 5300) 20km/12mi north-east on a spur above the estuary plain of the Cedrino, is dominated by the tall façades of the churches above crooked alleys and lanes. Surrounded by churches and chapels, the main square with its shady trees seem unchanged by time.

In the centre of town you'll find the hotel restaurant *su Barchile (10 rooms | Via*

Dunes and sand follow the coast to Cala Ginepro. To the north, is the breathtakingly beautiful INSIDER TIP nature reserve, *Parco Oasi di Bidderosa (entrance SS 125 km 236.5 | daily limit max. 400 people/160 cars)* with no less than five spectacular bathing coves.

SINISCOLA, POSADA AND LA CALETTA (125 F4) (*Ø G6–7*)

At ★ *Capo Comino*, some 40km/25mi north-east marks the beginning of the wide sandy beach, which only ends at

Drop by drop, nature creates a bizarre natural wonder: Grotta di Ispinigoli

Mannu 5 | tel. 0 78 49 88 79 | www.sub archile.it | Moderate). The enchanting INSIDER TIP *Anticos Palathos (9 rooms and suites | Via Nazionale 51 | tel. 0 78 49 86 04 | www.anticospalathos. com | Expensive)* in the historic centre is one of the most beautiful hotels in Sardinia. The charmingly labyrinthine palazzo with its green atrium, all furnished in the old Sardinian style, will transport you to a bygone era.

A broad pine-fringed sandy beach extends between the estuary of the Cedrino and Osalla bay; beach hikers with stamina will find splendid isolation here.

Posada, the former fortification guarding the border with the Gallura. Pine trees accompany the dunes, only giving way to shallow wetlands in the two wide river estuaries. Guarded by massive Saracen towers, the coastal villages of *Santa Lucia* and *La Caletta* are popular resorts.

The village of ☀ *Posada* with its castle occupies a scenic position perched on top of a rock hill. In the old part of town, the Hotel *sa Rocca (12 rooms | tel. 07 84 85 41 39 | www.hotelsarocca.com | Budget)* awaits. *Siniscola* lies more inland below the majestic limestone massif of Monte Albo.

THE INTERIOR

Compared with other mountains in the Mediterranean, the highest peak on Sardinia, the Punta La Marmora at 1834m/6017ft, in Gennargentu, is not particularly high.

The Gennargentu massif only turns into a giant in the context of its surroundings, the jagged limestone crags of the Supramonte in the north and east, the distinctive humps and valleys of the Barbagia Mountains of Ollolai in the north and the vast high plateaus and volcanic table mountains of the south and west.

Barbagia (land of the barbarians) was the pejorative name the Romans gave the mountainous country in the heart of Sardinia, one that they never managed to conquer. The subsequent rulers of the island also looked down with contempt and fear on the shepherds who, over the course of centuries, claimed the proud heritage of the Sardinians of being *barbaricini* – never subjugated nor assimilated into other cultures. Until the most recent past, written laws were not as important as the old traditional legal code, which regulated life in the villages and dealings with the outside world, with the principle of 'An eye for an eye, a tooth for a tooth'. This is why rejection of the state and its laws is one of the main themes of the *murales* in the Barbagia villages.

The walls, often dividing up the pastures in straight lines, unobstructed by valleys and slopes, can be seen everywhere. The leasehold rents are still a heavy burden on the shepherd families.

Photo: Monte Spada in the Gennargentu Mountains

A contrast to the coast: a scenic narrow gauge train ride, hiking Sardinia's highest mountain and the pastoral villages of Barbagia

ARITZO

(127 D2) (_E9_) Even in the height of summer, when all of Sardinia suffers heat and drought, the western slope of the Gennargentu remains a green oasis with dense chestnut forests and cork oak groves.

Situated at an altitude of 800m/2624ft, Aritzo (pop. 1700) is the place with the most springs in all of Sardinia and has traditionally been a summer resort that

provided a respite from the heat. Italian King Umberto I was one of the first to appreciate this. Today, Aritzo is famous for its chestnuts, for _Monte Tessile_ – a conspicuous rock used by the Nuragic as a place of worship – and also for the _sa Muvara Hotel (61 rooms | tel. 07 84 62 93 36 | www.samuvarahotel. com | Moderate–Expensive)_. The hotel is furnished with stylish art and crafts and is nestled on a slope on the southern edge of town in a spectacular location in a chestnut forest. Hotel owner Ninni

ARITZO

Paba is very active in preserving Sardinian art, culture and cuisine. Organic cuisine is on offer at the family-run 😊 *Agriturismo Mandaritzò (2 rooms | Via San Sebastiano 24/26 | tel. 07 84 62 92 72 | Budget–Moderate)* in the neighbouring village of Belvi.

PUNTA LA MARMORA ⭐ ☀
(127 E1) *(🗺 F9)*
South of Aritzo marks the beginning of the tarred high road which runs first through mountain forests then through mountain pastures to the ☀ *Arcu Guddetorgiu.* From there a road goes to Cuile

150 round huts and a citadel: the nuraghe fortification of su Nuraxi in Barumini

A mile or so outside Aritzo, amidst a wild romantic mountain landscape lies the once-important copper mine, *Miniera Funtana Raminosa (Mon–Fri 9am–1pm and 2.30pm–4.30pm, Sat/Sun 9am–1pm).*

WHERE TO GO

DESULO (127 D1) *(🗺 E9)*
Like other villages in the Barbagia, this mountain village 15km/9mi north-east is a stronghold of Sardinian culture and tradition. Elderly women still wear their colourful traditional costumes every day. Embroidered children's bonnets from Desulo are popular in the whole of Sardinia, as are its aromatic honey and sausages.

Meriagu and then a path leads up through scant oak forests and meadows to Sardinia's highest peak, the Punta La Marmora (1834m/6017ft), taking about four hours. Hiking up on the 'roof of Sardinia' takes you pretty close to the sky and on clear days you will enjoy some breathtaking views. While the hike is not difficult, do wear proper hiking boots.

SADALI (127 D–E2) *(🗺 E–F10)*
The small village 30km/18.5mi to the south lies on the edge of an extensive plateau. Its old houses are on steep, narrow roads on the slope below the new village. Alleyways lead to the gardens and the water mill in the valley, and the

sound of springs, brooks and waterfalls can be heard everywhere.

6km/3.5mi north-west is a *stalactite cave*, the *Grotte Is Janas (April/May and Sept/Oct daily 10am–1pm and 3pm–5pm, June–Aug 10.30am–1pm and 3pm–6.30pm | www.grottesadali.it)*. Excellent mountain cuisine can be enjoyed in beautiful natural surroundings near the cave at the *Is Janas Ristorante (same opening times as the cave | tel. 0 78 25 93 45 | Budget–Moderate)*. For accommodation, try the charming and environmentally-friendly ☺ *Monte Granatico hotel (13 rooms | Via Roma 53 | tel. 3496 93 93 18 | www.montegranatico.it | Budget–Moderate)*.

TONARA AND SORGONO (127 D1) (*Ⓜ E9*)

The road first follows the railway line, then it leads up through forests to *Tonara*. The village is famous throughout Sardinia for its sweet delicacy of *torrone*, made from egg white and nuts, as well as for the little bells made here for goats, sheep and cows, whose sound can be heard all over the island. Carpet weaving and woodcarving are other traditional crafts still alive here, and the main road is lined with modern wooden statues by a local folk artists. The INSIDER TIP ▶ Locanda su Muggianeddu *(closed Fri | tel. 0 78 46 38 85 | Budget)* provides hearty traditional fare; diners can stay the night in seven simple guest rooms.

The neighbouring little town of *Sorgono* is famous for its Mandrolisai, a top-class red wine which is only cultivated around Sorgono. A good reason for wine lovers to visit the *Cantina del Mandrolisai (Corso IV Novembre 20 | www.mandrolisai.com)*. An inexpensive place to eat and stay the night is just a few paces away, the *Da Nino* hotel restaurant *(17 rooms | Corso IV Novembre 26 | tel. 0 78 46 01 27 | Budget)*, famous for its excellent food.

BARUMINI

(126–127 C–D3) (*Ⓜ E10*) **In 1949, following days of rain, a hillside started sliding, revealing ancient walls and foundations.**

The ★ *su Nuraxi nuraghe fortification (daily 9am–one hour before sunset)* was once a castle and the seat of a mighty tribal fiefdom. The citadel, with four corner towers and a central tower, was surrounded by a thick turreted wall; some of the 150 round huts of the village outside – still clearly visible today – served as workshops.

★ **Punta La Marmora**
Hike to the highest point of Sardinia – the views seem endless
→ p. 86

★ **su Nuraxi nuraghe fortification**
The walls and defensive towers of this complex were constructed in the Nuragic era with massive stones → p. 87

★ **Giara di Gesturi**
Uninhabited basalt plateau where wild horses and other wildlife roam free → p. 88

★ **su Gologone**
The mightiest spring of the island arises at this pretty hotel near Oliena → p. 92

★ **Murales in Orgosolo**
The numerous wall murals, painted in different styles, have turned the town into a large outdoor gallery → p. 93

MARCO POLO HIGHLIGHTS

BARUMINI

The oldest parts of the settlement, such as the central tower, still date from the early Nuragic era around 1200 BC. Most of the walls and towers however are 200 to 400 years younger, whilst most of the village itself dates from the later Nuragic era, when the Punics had already conquered this part of the island and the lords of su Nuraxi were probably their vassals.

WHERE TO GO

GIARA DI GESTURI ★ ☼
(126–127 C–D2) (*m D–E10*)
The basalt plateau is 12km/7.5mi long and about 5km/3mi wide and covered with maquis and cork oaks. In winter, large bodies of water form on the impermeable basalt. In addition to goats, sheep and semi-wild domestic pigs, around 1500 horses live here in complete freedom. Several roads lead to the high plateau; the best places to start from are *Gesturi* and *Tuili* with its magnificent baroque church. Once up there, the only way to continue on is on foot or by bike.

GIARA DI SERRI (127 D3) (*m E10*)
This basalt plain lies opposite and is much smaller, more barren and rugged. Access is via the shepherd's village of Serri. At the front end of the plateau, where the *Santa Vittoria* chapel seems to float above the low hill country of the Marmilla, lies the *Santuario Nuragico Santa Vittoria (daily 9am–7pm, Nov–March to 5pm)*. It was probably a kind of prehistoric Olympia, with temple area and oval sports ground, where brave men toughed it out in tournaments. Particularly impressive is the very well preserved subterranean well sanctuary, its layout closely resembling the one at Santa Cristina.

ISILI AND LACONI (127 D2) (*m E10*)
Between Giara and Gennargentu, is the bare Sarcidano, a rugged limestone plateau with fissured by deep gorges. *Isili* is famous for its beautiful copper and

Over 1500 wild horses roam free on the basalt plateau of Giara di Gesturi

weaving crafts (*Museo del Rame e del Tessuto* | *Tue–Sun 10am–1pm and 4.30pm–7pm* | *www.rametessuto.com*). The nuraghe of *is Paras* (*April–Oct Tue–Sun 10am–1pm and 4.30pm–7.30pm, Nov–March 10am–1pm and 3pm–5pm*) along the road leading north is the only one on Sardinia constructed from white limestone.

Laconi is where the Capuchin monk Saint Ignazio was born and worked his miracles; deeply revered by the Sardinians, his image can be found in nearly every house on the island. The verdant *Parco Marchesi Aymerich* with the ruins of the Castello Aymerich is very beautiful and not to be missed is a visit to the *Museo delle Statue Menhir* (*daily except the first Mon in the month 9am–1pm and 4pm–7pm, in winter to 6pm*) which shows numerous menhirs mainly found in the area of Laconi. These monoliths from the Stone and Bronze Ages are partly adorned with reliefs, which make them resemble human figures and faces.

NUORO

MAP INSIDE BACK COVER

(125 E5) (*ℳ F8*) **The old town of Nuoro (pop. 37,000), which has kept much of its village atmosphere, is literally hidden behind fake Mussolini-era marble and very recent concrete.**

At the turn of the 20th century, Nuoro was still a small town, home to the owners of large herds and hired herdsmen. Thanks to the court, colleges, the prison and the bishop's see, this is now the largest town in the Barbagia. The aroma of sheep droppings on the streets only disappeared after 1927, when Nuoro became the provincial capital.

SIGHTSEEING

OLD TOWN

The *Corso Garibaldi* leading right into the heart of the old town is its only 'urban' street. At the end of the Corso, at the height of the tree-lined Piazza Vittorio Emanuele, a lane to the left leads uphill to the quiet INSIDER TIP *Piazza Sebastiano Satta,* dedicated to the memory of the Barbagia poet who was born in Nuoro. The large granite blocks on the square evoke prehistoric stone circles. Via Tola leads via the Piazza San Giovanni to Nuoro's neoclassical cathedral of *Santa Maria della Neve.*

MUSEO DELEDDIANO

The birthplace of the poet (Nobel Prize 1926) gives a good idea of the lifestyle and living conditions of a wealthy family around the year 1900. *Via Grazia Deledda 42* | *mid March–mid June Tue–Sun 9am–1pm and 3pm–6pm, mid June–Sept daily 9am–7pm, Oct–mid March Tue–Sun 10am–1pm and 3pm–5pm* | *www.isre sardegna.it*

MUSEO ETNOGRAFICO SARDO ●

Also called *Museo del Costume*. Well documented overview of costumes and crafts from the Nuoro province, festivals and living conditions. *Via Mereu 56* | *mid March–mid June Tue–Sun 9am–1pm and 3p–6pm, mid June–Sept daily 9am–7pm, Oct–mid March Tue–Sun 10am–1pm and 3pm–5pm* | *www.isresardegna.it*

FOOD & DRINK – WHERE TO STAY

AGRITURISMO COSTIOLU ●

Pure unadulterated Barbagia! This estate with grounds covering nearly 250 acres is situated 10km/6mi outside the village along the road to Bitti (SS 389 km 90) amidst remote nature. Experience the authentic taste of the Barbagia, nearly everything is home-made on the property and can also be purchased. Cookery courses are also available. *10 rooms | tel. 0784 26 00 88 | www.agri turismocostiolu.com | Moderate–Expensive*

GRILLO

This mid-range hotel with good restaurant is a centrally located. *45 rooms | Via Monsignor Melas 14 | tel. 0 78 43 86 78 | www.grillohotel.it | Moderate*

LOW BUDGET

▶ In Sadali, on the southern edge of the Barbagia, you can enjoy inexpensive meals with generous portions at the *Trattoria su Stori (closed Tue | tel. 0 78 25 90 42)*.

▶ For very little money you can enjoy simple accommodation and good food in Desulo at the *Locanda La Nuova (7 rooms | tel. 0784 61 92 51)*.

▶ For an inexpensive stay in a scenic setting try the idyllic *Supramonte* campsite *(Sarthu Thitthu | tel. 0784 40 10 15 | www.supramonte.it)* near Orgosolo. The traditional Barbagian fare served up at the *ristorante* is also very reasonably priced.

▶ The *Ostello Castagneto (65 beds in 12 rooms | tel. 0784 61 00 05)* in the mountain village of Tonara scores with cheap prices and its pretty location right in the village.

RIFUGIO

Excellent regional cuisine at reasonable prices and tasty pizzas make this old town trattoria a favourite meeting point for the locals. *Closed Wed | Via Mereu 28 | tel. 0784 23 23 55 | www.trattoriarifugio.com | Budget*

SHOPPING

INSIDERTIP ISOLA

Carpets from the Barbagia, embroidered silk scarves from Oliena, gold filigree jewellery and replicas from Nuoro and Dorgali, and leather, in both traditional and modern designs. *Via Monsignor Bua 10 (near the cathedral)*

INFORMATION

Piazza Italia 19 | tel. 0784 23 88 78 | www.comune.nuoro.it, www.provincia.nuoro.it

WHERE TO GO

FONNI AND GAVOI (125 D6) *(ᗰ E8–9)*
Fonni 30km/18.5mi to the south is the island's highest village. New buildings mingle with old natural stone houses. The village is a good base for excursions into the Gennargentu massif. For accommodation, try the *Hotel Sa Orte (27 rooms | Via Roma 14 | tel. 0 78 45 80 20 | www.hotelsaorte.it | Moderate)*, a lovingly restored granite palace right in the historic old town.

On the mountain road towards Desulo a side road branches off to �☼ *Monte Spada* (1595m/5233ft), which ends at the valley ski lift station. From here, a hiking trail leads to ☼ *Punta La Marmora* (return trip approx. five hours).

The neighbouring village of *Gavoi* has a pretty historic centre and is surrounded by forests and mountain pastures with tall oaks. The *Santa Rughe* restaurant (closed Wed | tel. 0 78 45 37 74 | *Budget–Moderate*) in the village serves delicious traditional fare, but also pizzas. At the nearby reservoir lake of *Lago di Gusana*, the *Agriturismo Fuego* (tel. 0 78 45 20 52 | *Budget*) offers two rooms, rural tranquillity and authenitic cuisine.

is *Ruggero Mameli* (Via Crisponi 19 | *www.mascheremameli.com*), whose workshop you can visit. Those wanting to take a closer look at the masks can do so at his private *mask exhibition* (Corso Vittorio Emanuele III | appointments tel. 34 77 71 79 31), where is has assembled

Popular picnic spot: Monte Ortobene with the bronze 'Il Redentore' sculpture of the Redeemer

MAMOIADA (125 D6) (𝄞 F8)

This remote rural village just under 20km/12mi south of Nuoro owes its fame to its dark carnival, since time immemorial the *mamuthones* (creatures hiding behind scarily distorted black masks, and hung with heavy bells and draped in furs) and *issohadores* (wearing colourful costume and hiding their faces behind white grinning masks) have taken to the streets. Find out more about this ancient ritual in the small yet very interesting *Museo della Maschere* (Piazza Europa 15 | Tue–Sun, June–Sept daily 9am–1pm and 3pm–7pm | *www.museodellemaschere.it*).

One of the last mask carvers on the island over 200 of these impressive works of art. When in Mamoiada, don't miss buying one of the award-winning wines from the *Cantina Giuseppe Sedilesu* (Via Vittorio Emanuele II 64 | *www.giuseppe sedilesu.com*). A charming place to rest your head, as well as inexpensive Barbagia cuisine, can be found in the *Locanda Sa Rosada* (6 rooms | Piazza Europa 2 | tel. 0 78 45 67 13 | *Budget*), whose rooms are furnished country-style with old antiques.

MONTE ORTOBENE ● ⚓
(125 E5) (𝄞 F8)

A winding circular road leads up Nuoro's 955m/3133ft high mountain. Many Nuorese make use of the shade provided by the trees and granite boulders to have their Sunday picnics here. At the top is a bronze statue of the Redeemer. The views down to the city and the mountains of the Supramonte and Gennargentu are unparalleled.

SARULE (125 D6) (∅ E8)

In many of the houses in this village 30km/18.5mi to the south-west you'll still find the high weaving looms where three or four women weave the carpets that have made the village famous. Classic, simple shepherd's fare from the Barbagia is served at the *Da Cannone* restaurant *(closed Sat/Sun | Via Togliatti 2 | tel. 07 84 76 0 75 | Budget)*.

OLIENA

(125 E6) (∅ F8) This charming mountain village (pop. 7700) is famous for its Cannonau red wine Nepente, its brightly embroidered costumes and its local specialities.

Thanks to its position at the foot of the highest Supramonte peak of Monte Corrasi (1463m/4711ft) and the pioneering work by the Enis cooperative, it has become a centre for trekking and other outdoor activities. While boasting a good tourist infrastructure, it has still managed to hold on to its authenticity.

FOOD & DRINK – WHERE TO STAY

CI KAPPA (CK)

Small cosy hotel in the centre. In the restaurant enjoy fresh pasta, lamb, roast suckling pig, game and mushrooms. *7 rooms | Corso Martin Luther King 2–4 | tel. 07 84 28 80 24 | www.cikappa.com | Budget*

INSIDER TIP ▶ ENIS MONTE MACCIONE

High above Oliena is the empire of this dynamic cooperative. Traditional cuisine is served in the shade of holm oaks. Ask for a room with access to the sublime roof terrace overlooking Nuoro! Hikes and climbing tours in the Supramonte are also on offer. *16 rooms | tel. 07 84 28 83 63 | www.coopenis.it | Budget–Moderate*

SU GOLOGONE ★ ●

Halfway to Dorgali, 8km/5mi to the east, su Gologone, the mightiest spring on Sardinia, breaks out here from the rock of the Supramonte and gives birth to the Riu Cedrino. Water taps provide cool drinking water and a small bar has drinks

FAMILY FEUDS

Vendettas and family feuds that could last for decades were still prevalent in the interior up until about the middle of the 20th century. Where the state intervened and tried to enforce its norms, new conflicts arose and the existing ones became worse. The police and special units searched for murderers who, in the eyes of the Sardinians, had only done their duty by the family honour. Even spies were used. Negotiations between warring parties were no longer possible. As the wanted men disappeared as outlaws into the mountains, the spiral of violence went on.

and snacks. A heavenly place to relax! Known all over the island, the hotel is furnished with Sardinian antiquities and crafts. *72 rooms | tel. 07 84 28 75 12 | www.sugologone.it | Expensive*

WHERE TO GO

ORGOSOLO ● (125 E6) *(Ω F8)*

15km/9mi to the south is Sardinia's most famous village (pop. 4800) – it is even on

poverty and repression, police, bureaucracy and the military – in naïve art style, Sardinian's *murales* have become world famous. Collaborating with professional artists, the villagers have created the ★ *murales* themselves, constantly taking up new issues. A modest hotel in the centre, that also serves good food, is the *Petit Hotel (18 rooms | tel. 07 84 40 33 13 | mar.or@tiscali.it | Budget)*, a meeting place for young people.

Murales: the expressive murals on the walls in Orgosolo depict Sardinian history and issues

the itinerary of the large tour buses – as this is the area of vendettas, bandits and rebellion against the state. At first glance, Orgosolo appears a fairly normal village with plenty of new buildings. What seems unusual however are the large police barracks and the many *murales,* even in the hidden back alleys. The murals are a clear expression of the social concerns of the locals: unemployment and emigration, the social situation of the shepherds, the discrimination of the Sardinians in their own country, the arrogance of the politicians. Painted on to house walls – as a graphic protest and accusation against

A narrow road leads across the wild, romantic plateau of Pratobello into the INSIDER TIP *Foresta di Montes,* one of the most beautiful and pristine areas of the Barbagia. The road ends at a forest station with information point. From here there is an uphill walk through the forest to the *Funtana Bona* spring with picnic facilities, and futher on to the striking ☆ rock needle of *Monte Novo San Giovanni* (1316m/4317ft). This can be accessed by a path of stairs hewn into the rock (approx. 2 hours return trip from the forest station). The panoramic views from the top are sensational.

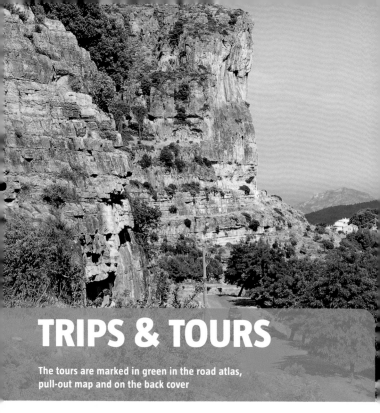

TRIPS & TOURS

The tours are marked in green in the road atlas,
pull-out map and on the back cover

1 FROM ALGHERO INTO THE MAGICAL FOREST OF BADDE SALIGHES

This tour leads from the sea fairly quickly uphill to the Campeda plateau, allowing you to admire plenty of ancient nuraghi, menhirs and *domus de janas* along the way. The final destination of the tour is the forest of Badde Salighes, a wonderfully cool green oasis in summer. Allow yourself two days for this tour of approx. 160km/100mi.

Immediately after Alghero → p. 44, the serpentine road wends its way up to the top of Scala Piccada where, at an altitude of 355m/1165ft, you can see a large part of northwest Sardinia at your feet. The route to the village of Villanova Monteleone, famous for its carpet and blanket weaving, leads through isolated forest and scrubland, where semi-wild domestic pigs roam. Visible from afar, 644m/2113ft Monte Minerva provides an unmistakable landmark. Like the other table mountains and the expansive high plains, this mountain is volcanic in origin. The houses of Monteleone Rocca Doria, dominated by the remains of the walls of the Genovese castello that gave the village its name, huddle close together on a conical mountain above the Temo reservoir lake.

Now the landscape opens up. Fields alternate with pastures, and the villages are close together, which is unusual for Sardinia. Also, they are large settlements, and their churches and monasteries tell

Visit nuraghi and the lush green mountains: breathtaking landscape and ancient sanctuaries which make history come alive

of better times. For a fine overview, head for the isolated pilgrimage church in the mountains on Monte Bonu Ighinu, which your reach by making a 3km/1.8mi detour on a tarmac road. A little further on, a good place to stop for food in Padria is the Locanda Zia Giovanna *(closed Sat | Via Fratelli Sulis 9 | tel. 0 79 80 70 74 | Budget)*. In neighbouring Pozzomaggiore, discover the impressively large Catalan Gothic parish church; before you reach the village you'll see the tiny San Nicolò di Trullas country church along

the road to Semestene; it was built by Tuscan master builders in the 13th century.

Now you reach the high plain of Campeda (roughly 30km/19mi long, between 10km/6mi and 12km/7.5mi wide, and between 500m/1640ft and 700m/2300ft high) that forms a natural bastion dividing the north from the south of Sardinia. Here – and in the Valle dei Nuraghi between Bonorva and Ittireddu to the north and the southerly, high Abbasanta plateau, lying 200m/656ft lower – is

The well preserved nuraghe of Santa Sabina standing in the plain at Silanus

the **Hotel Marghine** *(Restaurant Da Gigi | closed Sun | 15 rooms | Via Vittorio Emanuele 3 | tel. 0 78 57 07 37 | www.hotel marghine.it | Budget)* in **Macomer** → p. 52.

The next day, leave Macomer and head towards San Leonardo/Monte Sant'Antonio and take a right turn after a mile or so on to a single-track tarmac road that will lead you straight to the INSIDER TIP **Zona Archeologica di Tamuli** *(June–Sept Tue–Sun 10am–1pm and 3pm–7pm)*, including not only a nuraghe and three well preserved giant tombs, but also the **Sei Betili**, six conical stone figures, as strange as they are mysterious, facing each other in groups of three. As three of them display breast-like protrusions, they are thought to be female, the others male.

Borore is situated further down on the high plain. The well preserved **Nuraghe Imbertighe** and a large giant tomb, also well preserved, are reached from the ring road on the exit to Sedilo. The next two settlements, **Bortigali** and **Silanus,** nestle below the 800m/2624ft steep slope of the Marghine chain, and both are charming, quiet villages with gardens and small houses. In Silanus, the small Romanesque church of San Lorenzo with a phallic menhir in front is worth seeing, and in the plain, the **Santa Sabina** → p. 52 is a magical place with a small early Christian church right next to a mighty nuraghe.

In Bolotana, the road rises up into the mountains, providing ample water and shade. At the top of the pass, a road forks off to the left, leading to **Badde Salighes.** The 'valley of the willows' is a shallow depression on the Campeda plateau, a green oasis with holm oaks, junipers and yews – some of the oldest trees in Europe – as well as clear springs which in attract hundreds of Sardinians in summertime. Up here, not far from the highest point of

more evidence from prehistory than all the rest of Sardinia: nuraghi, temples, menhirs, giant tombs and fairy grottoes *(domus de janas)*. The area has been shaped over thousands of years by shepherds: pastures with a scattering of trees, usually cork and holm oaks, their crowns bent eastwards into bizarre shapes by the eternally blowing westerly wind. The drystone *tancas* walls so typical of Sardinia divide the huge expanses; many crossroads and watering points feature nuraghi and Christian churches, often in ancient pagan sites of worship. You can see this by the stone circles, usually several millennia older, which haven't all fallen victim to the zeal of monks and village priests. A good Sardinian meal and a bed for the night in pleasant, traditionally furnished rooms is on offer at

the Olbia–Cagliari railway line, the head of the construction works, English engineer Benjamin Piercy, once built his villa, planting trees from distant continents, which over the course of 130 years have become giants.

The nearby pilgrimage church of Santa Maria di Sauccu stands at an altitude of 845m/2772ft under tall oak trees and is surrounded by *cumbessias*, small houses where the pilgrims can stay for a few days, when the Madonna is celebrated on her feast day in the first half of September.

2 TRAVELLING THE BACK ROADS FROM CAGLIARI INTO THE GENNARGENTU

This tour, for which you should schedule a day or two, leads up for a good 200km/125mi into the wild mountain landscape of the Gennargentu massif. In addition to pre-Christian buildings and a cave, it is above all the rugged mountains and green river valleys that make this tour what it is.

First, the road from Cagliari → p. 59

heads towards Dolianova through the suburbs, and soon you're in the country-side. Dolianova is the main town in this region of rolling hills, which is Sardinia's main wine area, and boasts a large Romanesque cathedral. A detour via the neighbouring village of Serdiana and from there 3km/1.8mi in the direction of Sestu leads to the small country church of Santa Maria di Sibiola, which used to belong to a once powerful monastery.

The route now heads on northwards and the hills become higher and more barren. In Senorbì, the rich burial offerings found in the nearby Monte Luna necropolis – and now displayed at the archaeological museum of Sa Domu Nosta (*Via Scaledda 1 | Tue–Sun 9am–1pm and 4pm–7pm | www.museodomunosta.it*), housed in an old manor house – allow a glimpse of the world of the Phoenicians. The road now leads into the remote backcountry of the Gerrei to Goni, where the largest and most important prehistoric burial site in Sardinia, Pranu Muttedu Necropolis (*daily 8am–8pm, in winter 8.30am–6pm | www.pranumuttedu.com*)

Precious burial objects at the Sa Domu Nosta museum bear witness to the Phoenicians' cult of the dead

in a sparse cork oak forest. Amongst its particular attractions are the *perdas fittas*, long rows of menhirs, and two very well preserved circular tombs carved out of mighty blocks of rock.

● INSIDER TIP natural pool with shady trees, a meadow to sunbathe and picnic facilities. Dip into the wonderfully fresh water and then take a siesta!

Shortly beyond the natural pool, below

The course of the Flumendosa forms several natural dams and lakes

Via Ballao in the lovely Flumendos valley – which remains green even in the summer heat – the road snakes up to the high plains formed by red, green and black trachyte, a volcanic rock marking the transition to the Barbagia Mountains in the heart of the island. Roughly 2km/1.2mi beyond Ballao, towards Escalaplano, a narrow concrete road turns off to the left, ending after a few hundred metres, where the river forms an idyllic loop (look out for a small wooden plaque with piscina naturale). Here the water of the Flumendosa, picturesquely framed by rocks, forms a charming

the road near the fork leading off to Goni, stop off at the **Funtana Coberta,** a well preserved subterranean sacred well dating back to the 10th century; twelve steps lead down to its chamber, and after rainy days the refreshing water bubbles forth again.

Deep valleys, today partly filled by long narrow lakes, cut through this deserted and barren highland which must have once been very important as a defensive line to the independent mountain Sardinians against the Punics and Romans, considering the number of water sanctuaries, giant tombs and nuraghi.

From Escalaplano, which is surrounded by deep gorges, the road first winds down in endless curves and then goes straight up again on to the deserted high plain of Su Pranu between the reservoir lakes of Mulargia and Flumendosa. Rising out of the plain, crisscrossed by *tancas*, the **Arrubiu** nuraghe *(daily 9am–1pm and 3pm–8.30pm, Nov–Feb to 5pm)* represents one of the island's mightiest prehistoric fortifications. Consisting entirely of layered red trachyte, the fortress once had a central tower (which used to measure 30m/100ft, today it's only 16m/50ft), exterior towers and bastions armed with embrasures, an interior courtyard with a well shaft and a wine press once used by the Romans. Feel free to clamber around and explore.

In **Orroli**, the Vargiu family have turned their 200-year-old original farmstead into the beautiful INSIDER TIP **Museo Ristorante Omu Axiu** *(March–Nov daily, restaurant only May–mid Sept by request | tel. 0782 84 50 23 | www.omuaxiu.it | Moderate)*. The homestead, grouped attractively around a large courtyard with a well, is a very interesting museum showing the old estate with all its facilities, workshops and tools in the original. In its *ristorante*, Mama Vargiu personally prepares tasty specialities of the region. Accommodation is in the guest house that is part of the estate, only a few steps away *(11 rooms | Budget–Moderate)*.

From the neighbouring village of Nurri, a partial dirt road winds 5km/3mi down to **Lake Flumendosa** where the shoreside hotel **Istellas** *(10 rooms | tel. 0782 81 20 14 | www.istellas.it | Budget–Moderate)* offers accommodation. In season this is also where a ● INSIDER TIP nostalgic paddle wheel steamer *(www.laghisardegna.it)* departs for trips on the lake.

The centre of **Sadali** → p. 86 has medieval houses, an old watermill and a small waterfall right in the village. It is just under a mile to the **Grotta de is Janas** cave *(June–Aug daily 10.30am–1pm and 3pm–6.30pm, April/May and Sept/Oct 10.30am–1pm and 3pm–5pm | www.grottesadali.com)*, a 200m/656ft deep stalactite cave (facilities include a car park, bar and snack bar). Those looking for a bed in Sadali, should opt for the ☼ ☺ INSIDER TIP **Albergo Monte Granatico** *(13 rooms | Via Roma 53 | tel. 32 97 42 91 99 | www.montegranatico.it | Budget–Moderate)*, a particularly inviting place with sublime views. The picturesque hotel, housed in two historic buildings, has been lovingly restored using ecological building principles. It is furnished with antique Sardinian furniture has been awarded the EU environmental seal of approval. The rooms are stylish, simple and pretty, the managers Veronica and Battista are as friendly as they are helpful, and the *ristorante* transforms organic products from the region into delicious delicacies.

Towards Seui, the landscape becomes more varied. Rock pinnacles, steep crags, springs, brooks and forests, with ancient holm oaks, yew trees and holly, form a green oasis in the **Montarbu nature reserve**. 9km/5.5mi beyond Seui, a small side road forks off towards Lago Alto Flumendosa and the Montarbu. The mountains of the Gennargentu rise up on the other side of the Flumendosa valley. Below the striking, 1293m/4242ft **Monte Perda 'e Liana**, whose summit, topped by a rock needle, is visible from afar, a track leads to the nearby pass, marking the start of paths up to the peak of **Monte Tonneri**, an easy hike lasting approx. an hour and a half. 12km/7.5mi further on, the road joins the SS 389 Nuoro–Lanusei at Lago Alto del Flumendosa.

SPORTS & ACTIVITIES

Sardinia boasts over 1800km/1120mi of coastline. Water sports such as snorkelling and diving, sailing and windsurfing can be enjoyed all around the island. There are also attractive hikes in the mountains of the interior.

In terms of outdoor sports, Sardinia offers a cornucopia of options. Do bring a bit of pioneering spirit, as there is a lot to discover still outside the two current outdoor centres of Dorgali/Cala Gonone and Oliena. Only fit and experienced hikers, gifted with a keen sense of orientation though should attempt to go it alone, as trails and watering points are usually not marked, und in the summer, the sun can be merciless. You're better off placing yourself in the hands of one of the local professionally trained guides working for the numerous cooperatives spread all over the island.

Detailed information on sports and sporting events can be found on *www.sardegnaturismo.it/en*, *www.sardinianplaces.co.uk* and *www.essentialitaly.co.uk*, for instance. Dates and events are also listed in the two Sardinian daily newspapers; see *www.lanuovasardegna.it* and *www.unionesarda.it*.

CAVING

Caving is a Sardinian speciality however, of the more than 3000 known caves on the island only a handful are accessible to visitors. Excursions into unexplored subterranean worlds can be arranged through the local caving clubs of the FSS

Wind and waves, mountains and boats: diving and snorkelling along the rocky coasts, hiking through gorges and along old mule trails

(Federazione Speleologica Sarda) or with outdoor cooperatives.

CYCLING

The rides from the coast up into the mountains are demanding, featuring climbs of well over 1000m/3300ft. Bicycles may be transported in most trains and many of the buses. The best contact for mountain and road bike tours in the north of Sardinia is *Gallura Bike Point (tel. 33 41 43 50 42 | www.gal* *lurabikepoint.com/eng/)*, run by a Sardinian-German team; in the south the best contact is *Dolce Vita Biketours (tel. 07 09 20 98 85 | www.dolcevitabiketours. com)*. Both providers work closely with each other, so that you will be very well looked after even if crossing the island. To download a comprehensive bike tour atlas featuring 24 detailed descriptions of routes check *www.sardegnadigitalli brary.it/index.php?xsl=626&id=202368*.

DIVING

Divers and snorkelers find ideal conditions on the island's rocky coasts, particularly in the sea at the base of cliffs which make the ideal habitat for sea life with hiding places, nurseries and good choice of food. Diving classes for beginners, advanced and professional divers on the most beautiful spots in the archipelago of the La Maddalena national park are arranged by *Orso Diving (tel. 07899 90 01 | www.orsodiving.com)* in Porto Cervo. For wreck and nature dives far down in the south east near Villasimius in the Capo Carbonara marine park, contact the *MM Diving School (Torre delle Stelle | tel. 070 78 67 18).*

GOLF

Golfers may play all year round on overall total of 13 golf courses, amongst them four 18-hole courses: *Pevero Golf Club (tel. 0789 95 80 00 | www.golfclubpevero. com)* on the Costa Smeralda is the most refined place to swing a club, *Is Molas (tel. 070 9 24 10 13)* on the southern coast near Santa Margherita di Pula is where international tournaments take place, while *Is Arenas Golf Resort (tel. 078 35 20 36 | www.isarenas.it)* on the western coast near Oristano is fairly new still. Last not least, the *Sa Tanca Golf Club (tel. 070 80 71 45 | www.golfsatanca.it)* is a 15 minute drive along the coast east of Cagliari in Quartu Sant'Elena. For up to date online information see *www.feder golf.it.*

HIKING & MOUNTAINEERING

Sardinia's mountains, the remote high plateaus and, particularly in the east, the impressive gorges of the Supramonte around Dorgali, Baunei, Urzulei and Ol-

iena are perfect for hiking. Hiking maps can be purchased from various websites such as *www.themapshop.co.uk/europe/ italy/sardinia.htm.* However, as the trails are seldom marked, the best course of action is to join a guided tour with one of the trekking cooperatives operating island-wide. Recommendations include *Keya Tours (tel. 07849 82 95 | www.keya-sardegna.it)* in Orosei and the *Società Gorropu (tel. 33 38 50 71 57 | www.gorro pu.com)* in Urzulei, run by Sandra and Francesco (with an information point on the top of the pass at Genna Silana). In the mountains of Sulcis and Iglesiente, contact the *Società Start Uno (tel. 0781 58 09 90 | www.startuno.it)* in Fluminimaggiore, and in Sarrabus the Castiadas-based *Coop Monte Sette Fratelli (tel. 07 09 94 72 00 | www.montesettefra telli.com).*

HORSERIDING

The Sardinians love horses and are excellent riders, and there are now numerous opportunities across the island to explore the countryside on one-day or multi-day horseback excursions. Many *agriturismi* offer their guests this option. Great horse trekking tours along the Costa Verde are on offer by *Maneggio Cabus de Figus stables (tel. 0 78 15 49 43)* near Fluminimaggiore. For the best riding on the Costa del Sud contact *Maneggio di Giancarlo Cabras (tel. 07 09 23 60 45 | www.cavalcareachia. it).* In the north, Alessandro of *Terranur-agica (tel. 33 41 43 50 42)* organises fantastic tours through the Gallura for experienced riders. Recommended options on the Costa Rei are the *Centro Ippico Sar-rabus (tel. 0 70 99 90 78 | web.tiscali.it/ agriturismosarrabus),* and on the east coat try the *Associazione Ippica Montalbo (tel. 07 84 85 41 16 | www.posadacavallo. it)* – with a good B & B.

KAYAK

When the seas are calm, the steep coast in the east between Orosei, Cala Gonone and Santa Maria Navarrese makes an ideal terrain for trips by kayak as they are small enough to enter the narrowest fjords, smallest coves and sea caves.

farthest north, have well equipped marinas. An up-and-coming sailing area in the north-west is the Gulf of Asinara with ports in Castelsardo, Stintino and Alghero. For more information, see *www.sailingsardinia.co.uk,* where you may also hire yachts and sailing boats of various categories.

Divers love exploring the rocks of the sea floor, such as here at Capo Carbonara

Guided kayak tours around the island are arranged by *Sea Kayak Sardinia (tel. 36 64 97 96 71 | www.seakayaksardinia. com)*. For canoe and kayak tours on the Riu Coghinas near Valledoria, not far from Castelsardo, contact *New Kayak Sardinia (tel. 33 81 25 84 03 | www.newkayaksardinia.it)*.

SAILING & BOAT CHARTER

The entire Gallurese coast is ideal for sailing. The Costa Smeralda, the islands forming part of the national parks of La Maddalena, as well as Capo Testa in the

WINDSURFING

The wind-swept coasts of the north are best suited for windsurfing, particularly between Olbia and Castelsardo (the trendy choice is *Porto Pollo* near Palau), but the flat beaches of the west also offer good conditions, at Stintino and Alghero, on the Sinis Peninsula (Capo Mannu, Putzu Idu, Funtana Meiga) and on the Costa Verde. Top spots in the south can be found in the area around Torre Chia and Capo Carbonara near Villasimius.

TRAVEL
WITH KIDS

When it comes to children, the Sardinians make an exception and become very Italian: they just love children. They'll do anything for the bambini, even if they're not their own. And the parents are included in this open display of warmth and sympathy. Sardinia can offer children fantastic holiday experiences, far more than just beach and ice-cream parlour.

Apart from the Lunapark – with its merry-go-round and stalls of colourful plastic toys like those you can find at most holiday seaside resorts – there are hardly any facilities geared specifically towards children. But in high season nearly all campsites, holiday resorts and many hotels have a wide choice of entertainment activities and fun things for children to do.

Particularly popular with families is the very personal *Camping Capo Ferrato (tel. 0 70 99 10 12 | www.campingcapoferrato. it)* right behind the beach on Costa Rei, as the young creative manager Patrizia is always coming up with new ideas for her guests, big or small. Also very popular with young families is the small *Camping Sa Prama (tel. 0 78 49 10 72 | www.sapra ma.it)* in Cala Liberotto, boasting a direct access to a picture-perfect and toddler-friendly beach cove.

Leisure options specifically for adolescents are on offer at the Gulliver Camp run by *Camping La Foce (tel. 0 79 58 21 09 | www.lafoce.eu)* in Valledoria. *Amfibie Treks (tel. 3 83 48 38 38 70 | www.amfibietreks.co.uk)* with its two sites near Santa Lucia has also tailored its

Sandy beaches and mountain picnics: Sardinia's many fine sandy coves make ideal bathing spots for children

concept with a broad range of sports and activities specifically designed for children and adolescents.

The luxurious *Forte Village* resort *(tel. 0709 21 88 18 | www.fortevillageresort. com)* on the southern coast offers children their very own little empire. Here the little ones are looked after throughout the day in their own special children's town; there is even a proper children's restaurant with furniture to match. At Italian restaurants, even five-year-olds are considered normal eaters and en-couraged to try each course. If your child would like a plate of spaghetti or some fish and nothing else, just explain to the waiter. And why not do as the Sardinians do and go on a picnic, best at the week-end when the countryside comes alive. There are flat beaches with fine soft sand and gentle waves, where children can swim, splash about and build sand castles in safety, yet not all Sardinian beach-es are like that. Being less exposed to the strong winds, the east and south coast are more child-friendly.

Ideal swimming spots for children are the extensive coves of fine sand on the north-eastern coast around *San Teodoro, Siniscola, Budoni* and *Orosei,* where the dunes often have shady pine groves. The smaller beach coves further south around *Santa Maria Navarrese, Bari Sardo, Marina di Gairo* and in the south-east on *Costa Rei* also have soft, fine sand. When the *Poetto,* Cagliari's city beach with its lido, is not in the thrall of full summer season, children will find its white sands a paddling paradise full of happy peers and ice-cream parlours. *Porto Pino* and *Porto Botte* near the island of Sant'Antioco are other spots suitable for toddlers on the more rugged west of the island.

The *Costa Verde* dazzles with its miles of sandy beach and high dunes. Take water and drinks, a picnic and a beach umbrella! Similarly endless beaches are waiting to be discovered in the north of the *Sinis Peninsula.*

Snow-white, with sand as fine as semolina, is the bathing beach of *Alghero.* On the northern coast, families particularly appreciate the long fine sandy beaches of *Valledoria.* In the north-east between *Santa Teresa di Gallura* and *Costa Smeralda,* deep bays with cliffs, islets and headlands protect against the heavy swell.

THE NORTHEAST

AQUADREAM (129 E2–3) (*𝄜 F4*)
This extensive pool landscape holds a wealth of wet entertainment for the whole family. *Baia Sardinia, Mucchi Bianchi part of town | mid June–mid Sept daily 10.30am–6pm or 7pm | 18 euros, children up to 1.30m/4.2ft 12 euros | www.aquadream.it*

THE SOUTH

MUSEO DEL COLTELLO SARDO ●
(126 B3) (*𝄜 C11*)
One of the most beautiful things to take home from Sardinia is a shepherd's knife made the traditional way by hand. In Arbus, the museum's founder, artist and knife maker, Signore Pusceddu, not only displays the world's largest knife (its weight 295kg/650lb and length 4.85m/16ft have earned it an entry in the Guinness Book of Records) but visitors can also watch him while he's working, as well as purchase one of this valuable pieces. *Mon–Fri 9am–12.30pm and 3.30pm–7pm | free admission | Via Roma 15 | Arbus | www.museodelcoltello.it*

THE EAST COAST

TRIP ON A NARROW GAUGE TRAIN
(127 D–F2) (*𝄜 F–G 9–10*)
Railway romance: trundling through the spectacular Wild West scenery on

a nostalgic narrow gauge railway is fun for the whole family. The most beautiful section for a day trip is the journey from Arbatax to Sadali. *Mid June–mid Sept Wed–Mon twice daily, mid Sept–Oct Sat/Sun once daily | return trip 23 euros, children 11.50 euros | tel. 0 70 58 02 46 | www.treninoverde. com*

INSIDER TIP **PARCO MUSEO S'ABBA FRISCA** (125 E5) (*ω G8*)
An ideal destination for families, this extensive area is verdant with plenty of waterfalls, ponds and babbling brooks near the Grotta di Ispinigoli at Dorgali. It includes a romantic old mill and farm, a blacksmith's forge museum, historic workshops and a turtle section. *On the road from Ispinigoli/Cartoe to Cala Gonone | June–Sept daily 9am–noon and 3pm–7pm | 7 euros, children up to 12 years of age 4 euros | www.sabbafrisca. com*

THE INTERIOR

SARDEGNA IN MINIATURA
(127 D3) (*ω E10*)
Sardinian version of Legoland near Barumini, with reproductions of monuments, folklore and interactive exhibitions, as well as a planetarium and astronomy museum. *Mid March–Sept daily 10am–sunset, Oct–mid March Sun 10am–5pm | 10 euros, children 8 euros, under 1m/3.3ft go free, planetarium/astronomy museum 3 euros extra | www.sardegnainminiatura.it*

WILD HORSES ON THE GIARA DI GESTURI (126–127 C–D2) (*ω D–E10*)
From Gesturi, Tuili and Genoni, single lane roads lead on to the high plateau. From the Tuili entrance it's only a short stroll to one of the pools, where you can watch the small wild horses. *Access free, but only on foot, bike or horseback | information and guided tours: Coop Sa Jara Manna | tel. 07 09 36 81 70 | www.sajaramanna.it*

Better than any climbing frame: the bizarre rock formations on Capo Testa

FESTIVALS & EVENTS

The Sardinians enjoy their festivals – which often last an entire week – coming out in their beautiful costumes to dance, feast and drink and guests are treated to genuine displays of hospitality. The old Sardinian traditions, from costumed processions to the wild equestrian tournaments and Sardinian poetry competitions, or the solemn and penitent Easter processions, at are firmly anchored in everyday life.

HOLIDAYS

1 Jan *Capodanno;* **6 Jan** *Epifania; Pasquetta (Easter Monday);* **25 April** *Liberazione* (commemorating liberation from fascism); **1 May** *Festa del Lavoro;* **2 June** *Festa della Repubblica* (Republic Day); **15 Aug** *Ferragosto;* **1 Nov** *Ognissanti (All Saints);* **8 Dec** *Immacolata Concezione* (Immaculate Conception); **25 Dec** *Natale;* **26 Dec** *Santo Stefano*

FESTIVALS

FEBRUARY/MARCH
▶ **Carnevale:** the Barbagia region hosts a wild masquerade, such as in Mamoiada and Ottana: a battle between man and the nature, banishing winter.

The ▶ **sartiglia** in Oristano is a colourful equestrian festival, for the past few years it has been repeated in summer.

MARCH/APRIL
▶ **Settimana Santa:** Easter week on Sardinia is still celebrated as a profoundly religious event. In many villages, the suffering and resurrection of Christ are honoured with passion plays.

MAY
Thousands of costumed revellers take part in Sardinia's largest ▶ **procession** between 1–5 May from the church of Sant'Efisio in Cagliari to Santa Margherita di Pula, plus many floats and horseback riders. From Cagliari the procession moves along the sea to the small town 30km/18.5mi away.

1–10 May: ▶ **San Francesco** in Lula on Monte Albo above the east coast remains a destination for numerous Nuorese, attracting entire families and clans from the town to celebrate. Food and drink for this ten day festival are donated and are offered to all comers.

Penultimate Sunday: ▶ INSIDER TIP **cavalcata sarda** in Sassari, after Sant'Efisio the largest traditional costume show in Sardinia

Equestrian games and processions: Sardinian festivals are a blend of joie de vivre, pagan myths and Christian faith

JUNE

Beginning of the month: ▶ *Sardinia Cup* on Costa Smeralda, international sailing regatta

JULY

Hundreds of riders and thousands of spectators take part in the ▶ *ardia* on 6 and 7 July, a breakneck horse race around the Sant'Antine country church near Sedilo.

AUGUST

▶ *Madonna pilgrimages:* mid August (and September) is when the major pilgrimages to the churches in the remote mountains take place. Once there, the stone houses around the church are occupied, tents and temporary huts set up, marking the start of a picnic in honour of the Virgin that goes on for days.

15 Aug: Feast of the Assumption, called ▶ *Ferragosto* in Italy, the whole of Italy celebrates, with costumed festivals taking place in nearly all the villages of the Barbagia region.

In Sassari and in nearby Nulvi, the ▶ *Candelieri* processions featuring giant wooden candles begin on the evening of the 14th.

In Bosa: ▶ *Santa Maria del Mare,* costumed boat procession from the town, on to the river to the estuary.

Penultimate weekend in August ▶ INSIDER TIP *Festa del Redentore* is celebrated on Monte Ortobene near Nuoro. Sardinians from the entire interior don colourful costumes and make their way to the festival held below the statue of Christ on the summit.

SEPTEMBER

First Sunday in September: ▶ *San Salvatore* in Cabras. Barefoot young people, carry the saint's image over 12km/7.5mi to a country church. The festival commemorates salvation from a Saracen attack.

LINKS, BLOGS, APPS & MORE

LINKS

▶ www.ditzionariu.org Online dictionary explaining Sardinian words and concepts in Sardinian and Italian and translating them into English and vice versa

▶ http://nativlang.com/sardinian-language/sardinian-basic-phrases.php Impress the locals, especially in the interior and the south, with a few words in their own language!

▶ www.karasardegna.com Ordering service for traditional products that showcase Sardinian gastronomic heritage. The company also has a physical sales point at Olbia airport

▶ www.italymag.co.uk/italy/place/sardinia Online magazine for lovers of all things Italian with interesting contributions on a range of topics from lifestyle and food to accommodation and cultural events

NETWORKS

▶ www.tripadvisor.com/Attractions-g187879-Activities-c5-Sardinia.html TripAdvisor's Sardinia site is busy and, if taken with a grain of salt, a useful research tool.

▶ www.facebook.com/pages/GalluraBikePoint-Cycling-in-Sardinia-Italy-Mountainbike-Roadbike/101408907540?sk=wall&filter=12 The facebook site for Gallura Bikepoint, the enthusiastic cycling pioneering operation

▶ www.sardisk.dk/sardinia2.html Extremely comprehensive meta-site listing links about Sardinia – from language and research institutions to art courses and multilingual online magazines

VIDEOS & STREAMS

▶ www.sardinia.world-guides.com/sardinia_videos.html Collection of video clips and movies on Sardinia

▶ www.tripadvisor.co.uk/LocationPhotos-g187879-Sardinia.html Photo blog with over 25,000 images and videos from the island

▶ www.sardegnadigitallibrary.it Wonderfully comprehensive Sardinia archives

Regardless of whether you are still preparing your trip or already in Sardinia: these addresses will provide you with more information, videos and networks to make your holiday even more enjoyable

VIDEOS & STREAMS

with sectors for music, image, video and books that you could spend ages in, just browsing and downloading content. A fantastic find! In Italian only.

▶ www.sardegnacultura.it/gallerie/video/ A treasure trove for fans of the island. Comprehensive audio and video library of the region of Sardinia organised by subjects. In Italian only.

▶ www.sardegnaturismo.it/it/multimedia Pretty and informative collection of touristic audio, video and image libraries and two webcams

APPS

▶ Sardinia Beaches Multilingual app guide to over 200 beaches – divided up into provinces – with pictures, information on facilities and on how to get there

▶ Sardegna Al Mare Interactive atlas of Sardinian beaches. Clicking on a pin reveals the description of the beaches in text and images

▶ iSmeralda A fast and simple app dedicated to Sardinia with over 3000 entries and 900 images on subjects such as beaches, food, restaurants, accommodation, ferries, wine, weather, etc.

▶ Sardinia Inside Out An iPhone and iPad app that is a cultural tour of the island - lace makers, Romanesque churches, festivals and much more

▶ Ricette Sarde 100 traditional Sardinian recipes in text and image

BLOGS & FORUMS

▶ http://forum.virtualtourist.com/forum-66-1-Travel-Sardegna-1-forum.html Active internet platform on Sardinia, user-friendly layout, and with plenty of traffic, so a good place to put up your questions

▶ http://twitter.com/secretsardinia/ The Sardinian-based writer with a penchant for red wine and swimming in deserted coves also has as website: http://secret-sardinia.posterous.com

▶ www.camping.it/english/sardegna/ A comprehensive campsite and tourist resort website with map, online ferry booking service, last minute discounts and campsite descriptions

TRAVEL TIPS

ARRIVAL

Some holidaymakers arrive via Switzerland and the St Gotthard tunnel or via France, taking the ferry from Genoa or Livorno. Less important are the ports of La Spezia and Piombino and Civitavecchia, requiring a lot longer drive. Those travelling in high season should make sure to book in good time, as the whole of Italy is on holiday at that time and the ferries are usually completely booked. Outside high season, there are numerous special offers, some of them very good value. However, they are usually offered only in small quotas, only for a short time or requiring travel via Corsica – save money by getting the information early!

The port towns on the Italian mainland all have a railway connection, on Sardinia you have the ports of Olbia, Golfo Aranci, Cagliari and Porto Torres. The Sardinian railway network is quite rudimentary: there is only one main line from Olbia to Cagliari which branches off to Porto Torres and Iglesias. To change from train to boat and the other way round, schedule at least two hours. www.trenitalia.com

In season some airlines offer direct flights. Easyjet (Cagliari, Olbia) and Thomson Flights (Alghero) leave from Gatwick, British Airways from Heathrow (Cagliari) while Ryanair departs from Stansted, Luton and Dublin (Alghero). Outside the season there are far fewer direct connections available. Prices vary a lot and change all the time.

All routes offer day and night passages (seven to ten hours), from the most important ports also fast ferries (taking three to five hours) without berths. The ideal option is a night crossing with a berth, allowing you to arrive early in the morning, well rested. In addition to the strike-prone state-run Tirrenia, the market is dominated by Moby Lines, Sardinia Ferries and GNV. In order to counter their pricing cartel, Sardinia founded the low-cost 'Flotta Sarda' in 2011. www.ok-ferry.com.

RESPONSIBLE TRAVEL

It doesn't take a lot to be environmentally friendly whilst travelling. Don't just think about your carbon footprint whilst flying to and from your holiday destination but also about how you can protect nature and culture abroad. As a tourist it is especially important to respect nature, look out for local products, cycle instead of driving, save water and much more. If you would like to find out more about eco-tourism please visit: www.ecotourism.org

CAR HIRE

The cheapest option is usually to book before you travel through a large travel operator or online through a rental car broker. Book early for high season, as there are only limited numbers of vehicles available! A small car starts at approx. 200 euros per week.

CONSULATES & EMBASSIES

UK HONORARY CONSUL IN CAGLIARI
Viale Colombo 160 | 09045 Quartu SE CA Italy | tel. 0 70 82 86 28

From arrival to weather

Holiday from start to finish: the most important addresses and information for your trip to Sardinia

US EMBASSY IN ROME
Via Vittorio Veneto 121 | 00187 Rome, Italy | tel. 0 64 67 41

CUSTOMS

Items for personal use may be freely imported and exported within the EU. Guidance amounts include 800 cigarettes, 90 l of wine and 10 l of spirits. Much lower allowances apply to US citizens.

DRIVING

The Italian traffic regulations are largely to identical to British and EU usage. Important exceptions: outside of town car lights must to be switched on at all times, and there has to be a reflective vest for every passenger inside the car, which in the event of a breakdown has to be worn on leaving the car. The speed limit in built-up areas is 50km/h (30mph), on main roads 90 km/h (55mph), on dual carriageways 110km/h (68mph), on motorways 130km/h (80mph).

Petrol stations are usually open between 7.30am to 12.30pm and between 3.30pm to 7.30pm but are closed on Sundays. However, nearly all have an automated machine where you can fill up using credit cards or cash. You pay first then fill up so be sure to hold on to the receipt in case of the machine malfunctioning!

EMERGENCY

– Police tel. *112*
– Emergency medical assistance and ambulance *tel. 118*
– Breakdown assistance (land line) *tel. 80 0 11 68 00*

– Breakdown assistance (from foreign mobile phones) *tel. 0039 03 92 10 41*

INFORMATION

ITALIAN TOURIST BOARD (ENIT)
– *1, Princes Street | London W1B 2AY | tel. 020 74 08 12 54 | www.enit.it*
– *630, Fifth Avenue – Suite 1965 | New York NY 10111 | tel. 0212 2 45 56 18 | www.enit.it*
– *10850 Wilshire Blvd – Suite 725 | Los Angeles, CA 90024 | tel. 0310 820 18 98 | www.enit.it*

TOURISM WEBSITES
www.sardegnaturismo.it, www.authentic-italy.co.uk/sardinia_information.php

INFORMATION IN SARDINIA
In addition to the head office *(Sardegna Turismo | Viale Trieste 105 | 09123 Cagliari | tel. 07 06 06 72 26 | www.sardegna turismo.it)*, each of the eight provinces has their regional office *(ufficio turismo)*:
– *Cagliari: tel. 070604241 | www.provin cia.cagliari.it*

BUDGETING

Coffee	0.80–1.60 £ / 1.25–2.50 $ *for an espresso standing in a bar*
Snack	1.60–3.20 £ / 2.50–5 $ *a panino with cheese*
Admission	0–5 £ / 0–7.50 $ *for museums, nuraghi and archaeological sites*
Petrol	approx. 1.20 £ / 2 $ *for 1 l super unleaded 95*
Bus	approx. 5 £ / 7.50 $ *for 100km/approx. 60mi*

– Carbonia-Iglesias: tel. 0 78 16 69 52 38 | www.provincia.carboniaiglesias.it
– Medio Campidano: tel. 07 09 35 67 00 | www.provincia.mediocampidano.it
– Nuoro: tel. 07 84 23 88 78 | www.provincia.nuoro.it
– Ogliastra: tel. 07 82 66 00 00 | www.provincia.ogliasta.it
– Olbia-Tempio: tel. 07 89 55 77 32 | www.provincia.olbia-tempio.it
– Oristano: tel. 0 78 33 63 8 31 | www.provincia.or.it
– Sassari: tel. 0 79 29 95 44 | www.provincia.sassari.it

Larger towns and popular tourist resorts also have a municipal information point, and nearly every community has an in-formation point usually staffed by volunteers called *Pro Loco*.

HEALTH

Your European Health Insurance Card (EHIC) entitles you to the same level of free medical treatment as at home, however only as dispensed by doctors and hospitals of the USL (Unità Sanitaria Locale). If you are required to pay you should ask for a list of treatments received in order to be reimbursed once back home. In season, larger holiday resorts offer the *Guardia Medica Turistica*, a medical service for holidaymakers. Visitors from North America and other non-EU countries should take out private insurance.

WEATHER IN CAGLIARI

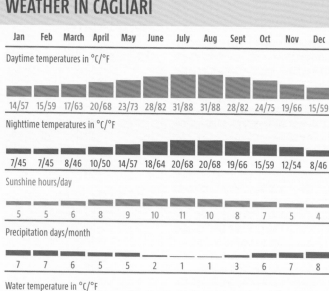

	Jan	Feb	March	April	May	June	July	Aug	Sept	Oct	Nov	Dec
Daytime temperatures in °C/°F	14/57	15/59	17/63	20/68	23/73	28/82	31/88	31/88	28/82	24/75	19/66	15/59
Nighttime temperatures in °C/°F	7/45	7/45	8/46	10/50	14/57	18/64	20/68	20/68	19/66	15/59	12/54	8/46
Sunshine hours/day	5	5	6	8	9	10	11	10	8	7	5	4
Precipitation days/month	7	7	6	5	5	2	1	1	3	6	7	8
Water temperature in °C/°F	14/57	13/55	14/57	15/59	17/63	20/68	23/73	24/75	23/73	21/70	18/64	15/59

IMMIGRATION

Citizens of the UK & Ireland, USA, Canada, Australia and New Zealand need only a valid passport to enter all countries of the EU. Children below the age of 12 need a children's passport.

INTERNET ACCESS & WI-FI

Sardinia has plenty of internet cafés. A good number of hotels and campsites have Wi-Fi (charging 2–5 euros an hour). Airports and some ferries have free hotspots.

MONEY & CREDIT CARDS

There are plenty of ATM cash points *(bancomat)*; credit cards are accepted by a great many hotels, restaurants, petrol stations and shops.

OPENING HOURS

On weekdays, shops are usually open between 8.30am and 1pm and between 5pm and 8pm, markets only in the mornings. In season numerous shops will stay open until 10pm or even midnight. Supermarkets and at least one bakery in each village are often also open on Sunday mornings.

PHONE & MOBILE PHONE

The international dialling code for Italy is *0039*, UK *0044*, US/Canada *001*. Italy has no area codes, so calling within Italy, the zero at the beginning of land line numbers always needs to be dialled. For tourists planning on frequent calls the best option is an Italian prepaid card. The SIM cards can be bought from network providers such as Tim, Vodafone or Wind; top-ups are available from numerous bars, kiosks, supermarkets, hotels, etc.

PUBLIC TRANSPORT

Sardinia has an extensive bus network. The state-run ARST *(www.arst.sardegna. it)* serves nearly every village on the island. There are also numerous private companies. Unfortunately there is no general schedule, nor are the services synchronised. All the larger towns have a municipal bus service and the major towns have a central bus station *(stazione autobus)*; in villages, the stop is usually in the centre of the village. Tickets can be purchased from bars, kiosks or from tobacconists around the bus stop *(fermata)*.

CURRENCY CONVERTER

£	€	€	£
1	1.10	1	0.90
3	3.30	3	2.70
5	5.50	5	4.50
13	14.30	13	11.70
40	44	40	36
75	82.50	75	67.50
120	132	120	108
250	275	250	225
500	550	500	450

$	€	€	$
1	0.70	1	1.40
3	2.10	3	4.20
5	3.50	5	7
13	9.10	13	18.20
40	28	40	56
75	52.50	75	105
120	84	120	168
250	175	250	350
500	350	500	700

For current exchange rates see www.xe.com

USEFUL PHRASES ITALIAN

PRONUNCIATION

c, cc	before e or i like ch in "church", e.g. ciabatta, otherwise like k
ch, cch	like k, e.g. pacchi, che
g, gg	before e or i like j in "just", e.g. gente, otherwise like g in "get"
gl	like "lli" in "million", e.g. figlio
gn	as in "cognac", e.g. bagno
sc	before e or i like sh, e.g. uscita
sch	like sk in "skill", e.g. Ischia
z	at the beginning of a word like dz in "adze", otherwise like ts

An accent on an Italian word shows that the stress is on the last syllable.
In other cases we have shown which syllable is stressed by placing a dot below
the relevant vowel.

IN BRIEF

Yes/No/Maybe	Sì/No/Forse
Please/Thank you	Per favore/Grazie
Excuse me, please!	Scusa!/Mi scusi
May I ...?/Pardon?	Posso ...? / Come dice?/Prego?
I would like to .../Have you got ...?	Vorrei .../Avete ...?
How much is ...?	Quanto costa ...?
I (don't) like that	(Non) mi piace
good/bad	buono/cattivo/bene/male
broken/doesn't work	guasto/non funziona
too much/much/little/all/nothing	troppo/molto/poco/tutto/niente
Help!/Attention!/Caution!	aiuto!/attenzione!/prudenza!
ambulance/police/fire brigade	ambulanza/polizia/vigili del fuoco
Prohibition/forbidden/danger/dangerous	divieto/vietato/pericolo/pericoloso
May I take a photo here/of you?	Posso fotografar La?

GREETINGS, FAREWELL

Good morning!/afternoon!/evening!/night!	Buon giorno!/Buon giorno!/Buona sera!/Buona notte!
Hello! / Goodbye!/See you	Ciao!/Salve! / Arrivederci!/Ciao!
My name is ...	Mi chiamo ...
What's your name?	Come si chiama?/Come ti chiami
I'm from ...	Vengo da ...

Parli italiano?

'Do you speak Italian?' This guide will help you to say the basic words and phrases in Italian.

DATE & TIME

Monday/Tuesday/Wednesday	lunedì/martedì/mercoledì
Thursday/Friday/Saturday	giovedì/venerdì/sabato
Sunday/holiday/ working day	domenica/(giorno) festivo/ (giorno) feriale
today/tomorrow/yesterday	oggi/domani/ieri
hour/minute	ora/minuto
day/night/week/month/year	giorno/notte/settimana/mese/anno
What time is it?	Che ora è? Che ore sono?
It's three o'clock/It's half past three	Sono le tre/Sono le tre e mezza
a quarter to four	le quattro meno un quarto/ un quarto alle quattro

TRAVEL

open/closed	aperto/chiuso
entrance/exit	entrata/uscita
departure/arrival	partenza/arrivo
toilets/ladies/gentlemen	bagno/toilette/signore/signori
(no) drinking water	acqua (non) potabile
Where is ...?/Where are ...?	Dov'è ...?/Dove sono ...?
left/right/straight ahead/back	sinistra/destra/dritto/indietro
close/far	vicino/lontano
bus/tram	bus/tram
taxi/cab	taxi/tassì
bus stop/cab stand	fermata/posteggio taxi
parking lot/parking garage	parcheggio/parcheggio coperto
street map/map	pianta/mappa
train station/harbour	stazione/porto
airport	aeroporto
schedule/ticket	orario/biglietto
supplement	supplemento
single/return	solo andata/andata e ritorno
train/track	treno/binario
platform	banchina/binario
I would like to rent ...	Vorrei noleggiare ...
a car/a bicycle	una macchina/una bicicletta
a boat	una barca
petrol/gas station	distributore/stazione di servizio
petrol/gas / diesel	benzina/diesel/gasolio
breakdown/repair shop	guasto/officina

FOOD & DRINK

Could you please book a table for tonight for four?	Vorrei prenotare per stasera un tavolo per quattro?
on the terrace/by the window	sulla terrazza/ vicino alla finestra
The menu, please	La carta/il menù, per favore
Could I please have ...?	Potrei avere ...?
bottle/carafe/glass	bottiglia/caraffa/bicchiere
knife/fork/spoon/salt/pepper	coltello/forchetta/cucchiaio/sale/pepe
sugar/vinegar/oil/milk/cream/lemon	zucchero/aceto/olio/latte/panna/limone
cold/too salty/not cooked	freddo/troppo salato/non cotto
with/without ice/sparkling	con/senza ghiaccio/gas
vegetarian/allergy	vegetariano/vegetariana/allergia
May I have the bill, please?	Vorrei pagare/Il conto, per favore
bill/tip	conto/mancia

SHOPPING

Where can I find...?	Dove posso trovare ...?
I'd like .../I'm looking for ...	Vorrei .../Cerco ...
Do you put photos onto CD?	Vorrei masterizzare delle foto su CD?
pharmacy/shopping centre/kiosk	farmacia/centro commerciale/edicola
department store/supermarket	grandemagazzino/supermercato
baker/market/grocery	forno/ mercato/negozio alimentare
photographic items/newspaper shop/	articoli per foto/giornalaio
100 grammes/1 kilo	un etto/un chilo
expensive/cheap/price/more/less	caro/economico/prezzo/di più/di meno
organically grown	di agricoltura biologica

ACCOMMODATION

I have booked a room	Ho prenotato una camera
Do you have any ... left?	Avete ancora ...
single room/double room	una (camera) singola/doppia
breakfast/half board/	prima colazione/mezza pensione/
full board (American plan)	pensione completa
at the front/seafront/lakefront	con vista/con vista sul mare/lago
shower/sit-down bath/balcony/terrace	doccia/bagno/balcone/terrazza
key/room card	chiave/scheda magnetica
luggage/suitcase/bag	bagaglio/valigia/borsa

BANKS, MONEY & CREDIT CARDS

bank/ATM/pin code	banca/bancomat/ codice segreto
cash/credit card	in contanti/carta di credito
bill/coin/change	banconota/moneta/il resto

USEFUL PHRASES

HEALTH

doctor/dentist/paediatrician	medico/dentista/pediatra
hospital/emergency clinic	ospedale/pronto soccorso/guardia medica
fever/pain/inflamed/injured	febbre/dolori/infiammato/ferito
diarrhoea/nausea/sunburn	diarrea/nausea/scottatura solare
plaster/bandage/ointment/cream	cerotto/fasciatura/pomata/crema
pain reliever/tablet/suppository	antidolorifico/compressa/supposta

POST, TELECOMMUNICATIONS & MEDIA

stamp/letter/postcard	francobollo/lettera/cartolina
I need a landline phone card/ I'm looking for a prepaid card for my mobile	Mi serve una scheda telefonica per la rete fissa/Cerco una scheda prepagata per il mio cellulare
Where can I find internet access?	Dove trovo un accesso internet?
dial/connection/engaged	comporre/linea/occupato
socket/adapter/charger	presa/riduttore/caricabatterie
computer/battery/rechargeable battery	computer/batteria/accumulatore
internet address (URL)/e-mail address	indirizzo internet/indirizzo email
internet connection/wifi	collegamento internet/wi-fi
e-mail/file/print	email/file/stampare

LEISURE, SPORTS & BEACH

beach/bathing beach	spiaggia/bagno/stabilimento balneare
sunshade/lounger/cable car/chair lift	ombrellone/sdraio/funivia/seggiovia
(rescue) hut/avalanche	rifugio/valanga

NUMBERS

0	zero		15	quindici
1	uno		16	sedici
2	due		17	diciassette
3	tre		18	diciotto
4	quattro		19	diciannove
5	cinque		20	venti
6	sei		21	ventuno
7	sette		50	cinquanta
8	otto		100	cento
9	nove		200	duecento
10	dieci		1000	mille
11	undici		2000	duemila
12	dodici		10000	diecimila
13	tredici		½	un mezzo
14	quattordici		¼	un quarto

NOTES

FOR YOUR NEXT HOLIDAY ...

MARCO POLO TRAVEL GUIDES

ALGARVE
AMSTERDAM
ATHENS
AUSTRALIA
BANGKOK
BARCELONA
BERLIN
BRUSSELS
BUDAPEST
CALIFORNIA
CAMBODIA
CAPE TOWN
  WINE LANDS,
  GARDEN ROUTE
CHINA
COLOGNE
COPENHAGEN
CORFU
COSTA BLANCA
  VALENCIA
COSTA DEL SOL
  GRANADA
CRETE
CUBA

CYPRUS
  NORTH AND
  SOUTH
DUBAI
DUBLIN
DUBROVNIK &
  DALMATIAN COAST
EDINBURGH
EGYPT
FINLAND
FLORENCE
FLORIDA
FRENCH RIVIERA
  NICE, CANNES &
  MONACO
FUERTEVENTURA
GRAN CANARIA
HONG KONG
  MACAU
ICELAND
IRELAND
ISRAEL
ISTANBUL
JORDAN

KOS
KRAKOW
LAKE GARDA
LANZAROTE
LAS VEGAS
LISBON
LONDON
LOS ANGELES
MADEIRA
  PORTO SANTO
MADRID
MALLORCA
MALTA
  GOZO
MOROCCO
MUNICH
NEW YORK
NEW ZEALAND
NORWAY
OSLO
PARIS

PRAGUE
RHODES
ROME
SAN FRANCISCO
SARDINIA
SHANGHAI
SICILY
SOUTH AFRICA
STOCKHOLM
TENERIFE
THAILAND
TURKEY
TURKEY
  SOUTH COAST
TUSCANY
UNITED ARAB
  EMIRATES
VENICE
VIENNA
VIETNAM

MARCO POLO
With ROAD ATLAS & PULL-OUT MAP
FRENCH RIVIERA
NICE, CANNES & MONACO
SPECTACULAR GRAND CANYON DU VERDON
Breath-taking scenery that takes some beating
SNIFFING THE AIR
The perfume manufacturers of Grasse
Travel with Insider Tips
www.marco-polo.com

MARCO POLO
With STREET ATLAS & PULL-OUT MAP
NEW YORK
MEADOWS, WILD FLOWERS AND SKYSCRAPERS
...is chic: the High Line in Chelsea
COCKTAIL ON CLOUD NINE
...rooftop bar at 230 Fifth Street
Travel with Insider Tips

MARCO POLO
...AKE GARDA
...ONTE BALDO WITH MOUNTAIN BIKE
...lar in Malcesine takes bikes too
...ISSES" IN SALÒ
...Cioccolato...Bacetto
Travel with Insider Tips

MARCO POLO
With ROAD ATLAS & PULL-OUT MAP
...ALLORCA
...AN FLAIR IN THE MEDITERRANEAN
...allorca's most beautiful beach
..." IN" CROWD MEET
...onita in Deia
Travel with Insider Tips

MARCO POLO
With STREET ATLAS & PULL-OUT MAP
BERLIN
A STUNNING ISLAND JUST FOR ART
...howcasing treasures from around the world
COOL AT NIGHT
...in club scene sets the trend
Travel with Insider Tips

- PACKED WITH INSIDER TIPS
- BEST WALKS AND TOURS
- FULL-COLOUR PULL-OUT MAP
  AND STREET ATLAS

ROAD ATLAS

The green line ▬▬ indicates the Trips & Tours (p. 94–99)
The blue line ▬▬ indicates The perfect route (p. 30–31)

All tours are also marked on the pull-out map

Photo: Capo Sandalo on the western tip of the Isola di San Pietro

Exploring Sardinia

The map on the back cover shows how the area has been sub-divided

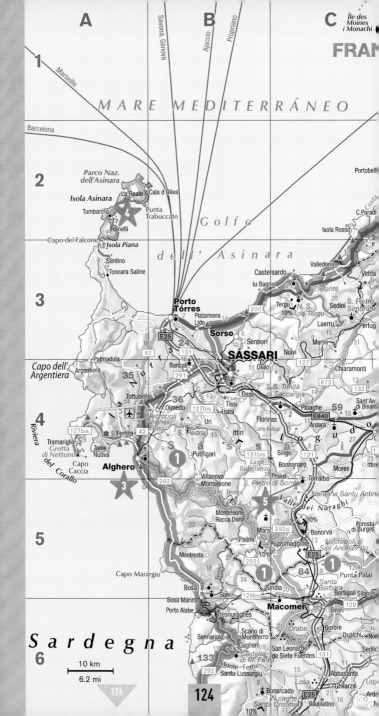

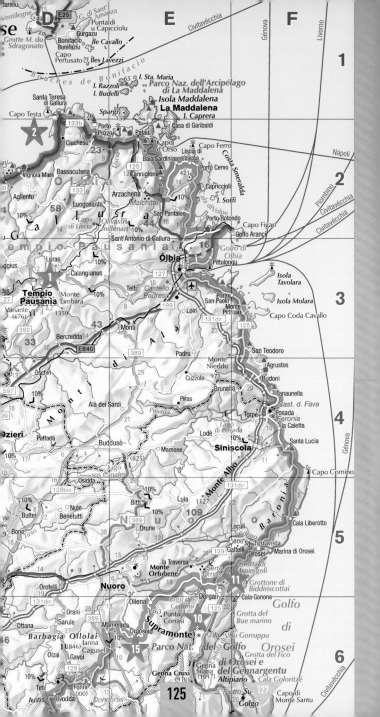

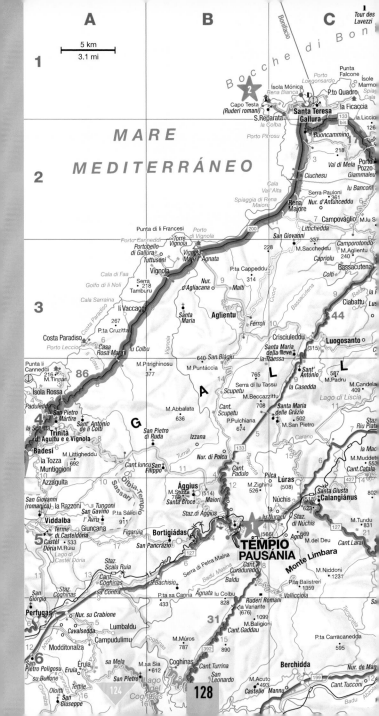

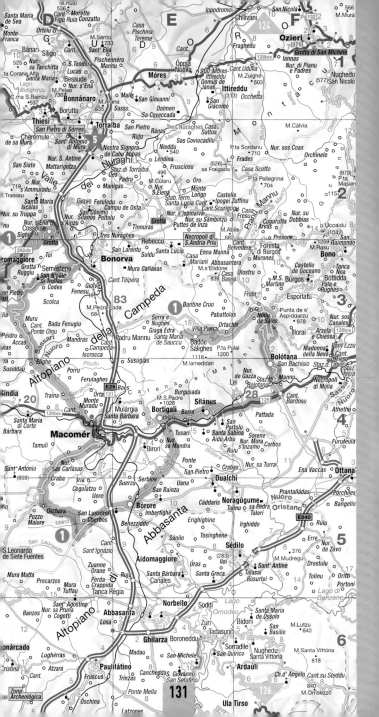

KEY TO ROAD ATLAS

18 26	Autobahn mit Anschlussstellen Motorway with junctions
	Autobahn in Bau Motorway under construction
I	Mautstelle Toll station
O	Raststätte mit Übernachtung Roadside restaurant and hotel
⊛	Raststätte Roadside restaurant
⊛	Tankstelle Filling-station
	Autobahnähnliche Schnell- straße mit Anschlussstelle Dual carriage-way with motorway characteristics with junction
	Fernverkehrsstraße Trunk road
	Durchgangsstraße Thoroughfare
	Wichtige Hauptstraße Important main road
	Hauptstraße Main road
	Nebenstraße Secondary road
	Eisenbahn Railway
🚃	Autozug-Terminal Car-loading terminal
	Zahnradbahn Mountain railway
⊢∘∘∘∘∘∘∘⊣	Kabinenschwebebahn Aerial cableway
....	Eisenbahnfähre Railway ferry
🚗	Autofähre Car ferry
- - - - -	Schifffahrtslinie Shipping route
	Landschaftlich besonders schöne Strecke Route with beautiful scenery
Alleenstr.	Touristenstraße Tourist route
XI-V	Wintersperre Closure in winter
×-×-×-×-×	Straße für Kfz gesperrt Road closed to motor traffic
8% <	Bedeutende Steigungen Important gradients
🚐	Für Wohnwagen nicht empfehlenswert Not recommended for caravans
🚐	Für Wohnwagen gesperrt Closed for caravans
☀	Besonders schöner Ausblick Important panoramic view

* * *Donnortei* *Terme* *di Casteldoria*	Sehenswert: Kultur - Natur Of interest: culture - nature
∿	Badestrand Bathing beach
☐ ☐	Nationalpark, Naturpark National park, nature park
	Sperrgebiet Prohibited area
♦	Kirche Church
♦	Kloster Monastery
♦	Schloss, Burg Palace, castle
Ⅰ	Moschee Mosque
♦ ♦ ♦ ♦	Ruinen Ruins
⚐	Leuchtturm Lighthouse
♦	Turm Tower
∩	Höhle Cave
∴	Ausgrabungsstätte Archaeological excavation
▲	Jugendherberge Youth hostel
♠	Allein stehendes Hotel Isolated hotel
⌂	Berghütte Refuge
▲	Campingplatz Camping site
✈	Flughafen Airport
✈	Regionalflughafen Regional airport
✈	Flugplatz Airfield
	Staatsgrenze National boundary
	Verwaltungsgrenze Administrative boundary
⊖	Grenzkontrollstelle Check-point
⊖	Grenzkontrollstelle mit Beschränkung Check-point with restrictions
ROMA	Hauptstadt Capital
<u>**CÁGLIARI**</u>	Verwaltungssitz Seat of the administration
	Ausflüge & Touren Trips & Tours
	Perfekte Route Perfect route
★	MARCO POLO Highlight MARCO POLO Highlight

INDEX

The index lists all places, beaches and destinations mentioned in this guide. National parks, nuraghi, beaches etc. can be found under their name. Page numbers in bold refer to the main entry.